TRAVELS WITH JUDY:
In Search of Steinbeck's America

Vicki Cain

For Joan! Happy Travels! Vicki Cain

For my parents, Patricia and Kenneth Cain

For opening my life to the magical worlds discovered by reading, the thrilling adventures of road travel, and the unconditional love of shelter mutts.

Route Map

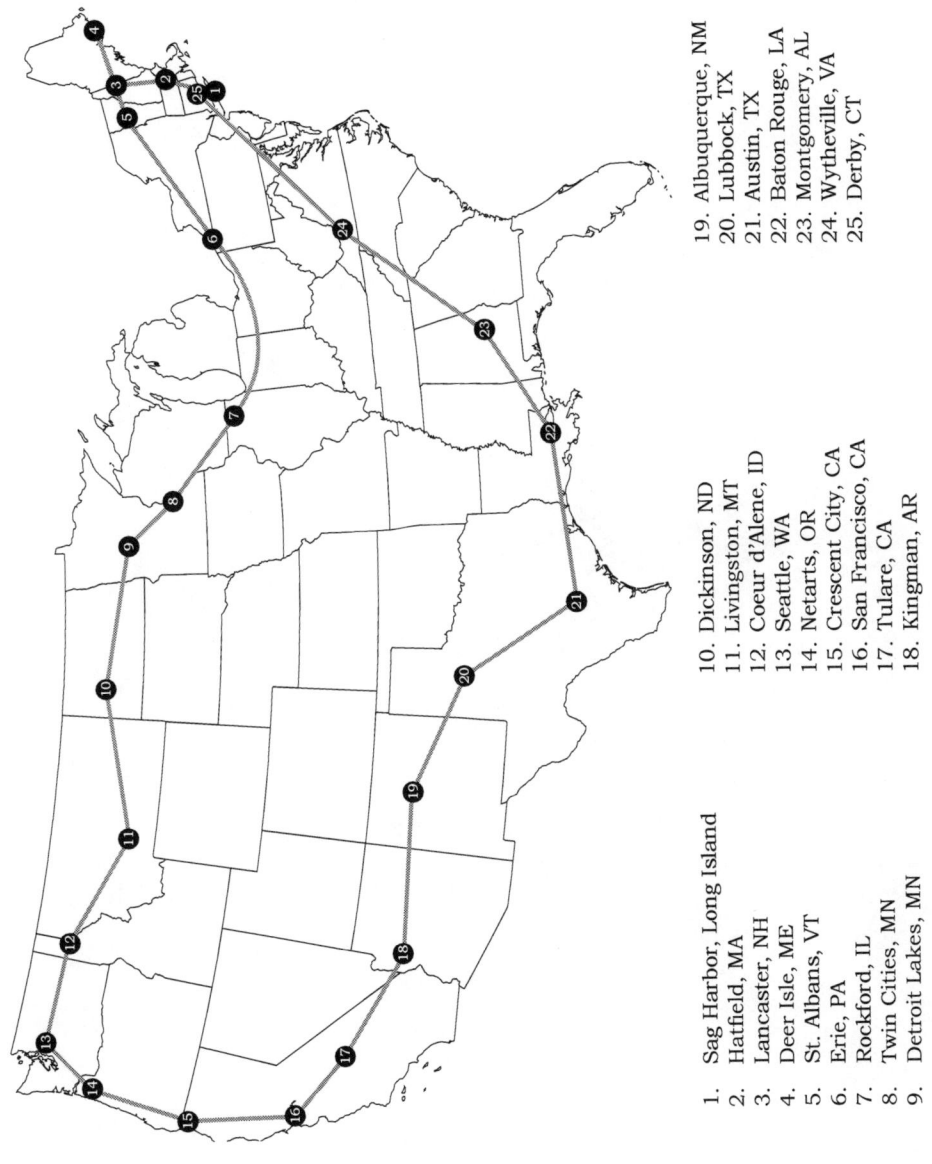

1. Sag Harbor, Long Island
2. Hatfield, MA
3. Lancaster, NH
4. Deer Isle, ME
5. St. Albans, VT
6. Erie, PA
7. Rockford, IL
8. Twin Cities, MN
9. Detroit Lakes, MN
10. Dickinson, ND
11. Livingston, MT
12. Coeur d'Alene, ID
13. Seattle, WA
14. Netarts, OR
15. Crescent City, CA
16. San Francisco, CA
17. Tulare, CA
18. Kingman, AR
19. Albuquerque, NM
20. Lubbock, TX
21. Austin, TX
22. Baton Rouge, LA
23. Montgomery, AL
24. Wytheville, VA
25. Derby, CT

Contents

PART ONE

Forget about necessity being the mother of invention, I'm convinced that boredom is the launchpad for more crazy impulses and bursts of genius than any accident, hard work, or just plain dumb luck.

In June of 2003, I was bored to sobs. One night during that late spring, I found myself rustling through my bookcase searching for reading material to help ease the dullness of the evening. I came across my ancient, yellowed, 1963 Bantam edition of *Travels with Charley—In Search of America* by John Steinbeck that I picked up at a garage sale some sixteen years earlier for seventy-five cents. It had been years since I had read it, and the idea of vicariously traveling along the back roads of America with John Steinbeck and his trusty poodle Charley sounded like the perfect escapist fare for the dull night ahead. I pulled it out of its place on the shelf, blew the dust off the top, opened its fragile pages, and as I had done several times before, settled in to enjoy the witty and wise thoughts of one of America's greatest writers.

Living in New York at the age of 58, John Steinbeck realized he was writing about an America that was, for him, only a distant memory. He hadn't traveled the country in 25 years and he said New York was no more America than Paris was France, or London was England. He decided to try to "rediscover this monster land," and so on September 23, 1960, he loaded up his custom-made truck camper named "Rocinante" (after Don Quixote's horse) and set off on a three-and-a-half-month journey with Charley by his side. His trip started in Sag Harbor, Long Island; took him to the potato fields of northern Maine; across New England to

Niagara Falls; through the Heartland in search of Sinclair Lewis; into the Pacific Northwest; down to his hometown of Salinas, CA; and across the Mojave Desert to Route 66. From there he turned back east and explored the Southwest, visited family in Texas, and witnessed seven-year-old Ruby Bridges integrating the William Frantz Elementary School in New Orleans—a moment that Norman Rockwell captured in his famous painting, *The Problem We All Live With*. Steinbeck marveled at the beauty of the Wisconsin Dells river gorge, and felt sorrow at the passing of regional dialects due to the influence of radio and television. Upon his return, he realized "the big and mysterious America is bigger than I thought. And more mysterious." The story of his road trip never ceased to entertain me, and with each reading I learned something new, so I was looking forward to being spellbound once again.

However, this reading turned out to be less fulfilling than I had anticipated. I didn't find the story to be as entertaining or humorous as on previous reads. I found myself rolling my eyes at some of Steinbeck's descriptions of the New England countryside and yawned at some of his observations of local personalities. This time, as I got deeper and deeper into the book, instead of feeling comforted by the words before me, I became more and more irritated. The following morning, after a late night of bothered and frenetic reading, I realized the source of my current dissatisfaction with this beloved story that I had read many times before—I was jealous. I wasn't content to just read about the trip anymore. Being an armchair traveler rather than a participant was clouding my enjoyment and forcing me to face my dissatisfaction with my currently stable and uneventful life wherein the largest excitement I'd recently had was finding a quarter in my couch cushions. The wandering itch had snuck up on me again. I knew I was in trouble.

What would it be like to take the trip today? Once this thought was planted in my head, it began to grow like a weed. The more I tried to put the idea aside, the more the idea turned over and over in my head and created nagging questions that couldn't be quieted.

In this age of the Internet, cable television, and cell phones, what has happened to the cheery melon stands, the friendly potato harvesters, and the desolate Badlands? Do they still exist? Has the capitalistic success of America driven the small ranchers, the traveling actors, and the fire-and-brimstone preachers into extinction? Is the racism Steinbeck experienced during school integration in New Orleans truly an embarrassing part of our not-so-distant past, or is it still present in less tangible forms? How far has the homogenization of our country really spread since the days when Steinbeck's camper bumped along those country roads with Charley eagerly riding shotgun?

I realized that the only way I could quiet the questions was to find out.

I put down my worn copy of the book and looked over at my dog, a ten-year-old, *bleu*-merle Australian Shepherd named Judy, and wondered if she might be up for such a journey. At the moment, she was peacefully lounging on her back with all four of her legs spread-eagled and her head hanging nose-down and half off the edge of the couch. While I looked at her, she took a deep breath, gave a mighty sigh, twisted her body into a half moon, and further extended her paws into the vast cosmos in a state of bliss.

What was I thinking? Judy might have come into my life after being incarcerated at the dog pound, but that didn't make her a tough and street-savvy bitch. On the contrary, she was a pampered indoor dog who didn't like to get her feet wet, and wouldn't even go outside when it rained. This was not a dog that would choose to spend weeks riding with her nose hanging out of the window in a camper instead of lounging on a large satin pillow surrounded by sugar cookies. She's more Dolly Parton than Sally Ride.

To complicate things, I remembered the times we had traveled together. Vague memories haunted me of one fateful day just outside of Laramie, Wyoming, when Chex Mix combined with carsickness caused Judy to daintily yet rapidly expel everything out of her system from both ends. Then again, she did give me a very memorable (albeit smelly) story to tell about Laramie...that is, if anyone should ever start a conversation about Laramie.

I decided to leave the decision up to her.

"What do you think, girl," I asked her. "Want to drive across the country?"

Still upside down, she opened one eye and gazed at me. When she saw that I was looking at her, she opened both of her eyes, bared her teeth in a grimacing smile and started pounding her tail against my arm. She was excited. I could tell.

I looked back at the book in my hand. Sure, I had traveled across the country before, but never alone, and never via back roads. Would we be able to do it? Memories of her carsickness washed over me, and for a split second, it seemed like too big of an idea. It was too far, too dangerous, too lonely...just too...everything. Then, just as I was about to file it away deep in the recesses of my mind under "harebrained ideas never launched" like the invention of a shower swing that I will never build, or the plan for the cookbook store that I will never open, I remembered Steinbeck's humorous account of Charley's first encounter with a giant Redwood tree, and that green-eyed monster made a second appearance.

On the other hand, I arrogantly justified, when was the last time Judy kicked her heels up and ran across a field unfettered or unfenced? She had never even chased a prairie dog or swum in a lake. Had she ever fallen asleep naked to the elements under the twinkling stars? She was a dog, for crying out loud! It would be a chance for her to explore her primal and wild canine self that had been suppressed in exchange for the life of the domestic goddess that she'd embraced for the majority of her years. She's going to love it, I thought, although I also had a twinge of doubt that maybe I wasn't being fair to Judy. Maybe I was really the one who wanted to fall asleep in an open field populated with wet prairie dogs, or something like that.

"You sure you want to go?"

She sneezed twice, twisted herself right side up as she flipped head-to-toe, slithered over to me on her belly and laid her head in my lap. She gazed up at me through her long, black eyelashes as I petted her on the head. Her tail pounded harder, and I took that as a big fat yes.

The Odyssey Begins

It was a dark and stormy morning.

September 18, 2004, dawned wet and wild as the remnants of Hurricane Ivan swept through coastal New England. Over four inches of rain were dumped on Connecticut before noon that day, and I thought of John Steinbeck and how he was originally supposed to leave on his journey just after Labor Day, but Hurricane Donna delayed his departure from Sag Harbor, Long Island, until September 23, 1960. The beginning of *Travels with Charley* details his crazy attempt to save his boat during the category 5 storm that affected every state on the eastern seaboard, and claimed 148 lives during its murderous jaunt. Comparably, Ivan caused 92 direct and 32 indirect fatalities and the hardest hit states were Texas, Louisiana, and Florida. Apparently, on the weather front at least, nothing much has changed in 44 years.

Regarding a vehicle, however, things had changed over the years. John Steinbeck had a three-quarter-ton pickup truck custom built with a camper top for his journey. Since 1960, camper trucks had become standardized and there were many options available to me. So many, in fact, I felt rather overwhelmed by the choices. I decided to defer the decision to some experts—my parents. When I was a kid growing up in southeastern Nebraska, we had a camper trailer that we used as a motel on our vacations. We'd find a campground that had all the amenities of a Travel Lodge, plug in the electricity, hook up the water, and connect our 2"x3" portable TV to the cable connection, hit the pool for a dip before dinner, and spend the night playing cards under the stars. Several members of my extended family also had campers, and once a year my aunts and uncles would drive the 40 miles from Lincoln to Beatrice to meet my grandparents and us at Riverside Park. Everyone would bring his or her camper and we'd stay for the weekend. Those weekends were some of the most fun and memorable of my life. During the day, my cousins, my sister, and I would go swimming, play ball, or hit the playground, while the menfolk would go fishing and drink beer, and the ladies would cook and talk. In the evenings we'd roast marshmallows and make s'mores while we sat bug-eyed in a semicircle on the ground around my grandmother's lawn chair while she regaled us with one of her many spooky ghost stories. One year, some other people at the campground dug a pit and roasted a pig all day. The delicious smell of the slowly cooking pork permeated every corner of the park, and to this day, I wish I could have eaten some of it. There really ought to be a law against public pig roasts if the public isn't invited. I always thought it was rather odd to go camping less than three miles from home, but no matter if it's three or three hundred miles, it's still an adventure.

My parents heartily embraced their commission and over Labor Day 2004, they drove out from their current home in Iowa and we spent the better part of a week cleaning, prepping, and stocking the 1978 Cruisemaster RV they brought with them. I named the RV "Roxie" which was a shortened version of Steinbeck's truck's name, "Rocinante."

Roxie was a 21-foot, class A motor home, with brown paneling and orange and brown shag carpeting that had seen better days. She had a Chevy engine and a leaky water tank, but considering she was 26 years old and had 76,000 miles on her, she was in excellent shape.

Inside, there were three double beds, a full kitchen with a stove, oven, fridge, sink, and cupboards. One of the beds was above the cab, one was a foldout couch, and the third was the breakfast nook. The stove, fridge, and heater were propane, and on the back of the vehicle was a gasoline-powered generator, in case I was ever camped at a place where there wasn't any electricity. This was particularly appealing to me because I had hoped to do a little bit of side-of-the-road camping like Steinbeck did and it would be nice to know I could have air-conditioning if it was unbearably hot. However, once we fired it up, it became obvious that the generator was basically useless. A Harley Davidson strapped to the back of the RV would have been quieter. The entire vehicle shook like a paint mixer while it was running. So much for modern comforts in rustic settings. It seemed that if the temperature rose, Judy and I were just going to end up being a couple of hot and sweaty babes for the night, or we were going to have to hit a motel for the evening.

All in all, I was thrilled with Roxie. I had always wanted a self-contained vacation unit, and I was already planning the many trips to Vermont we would be taking in the years to come once we got back from our journey. Judy, too, was extremely excited. When she first entered Roxie, she immediately jumped into the breakfast nook and sat at the table. After looking around a bit, she jumped on top of the table, hopped onto the seat on the other side, shook her head from side to side, then jumped to the floor and back into the first seat and flopped on her back for a belly rub with her tail pounding. I hadn't seen her look that overjoyed in years! This was going to be a great trip.

Once Roxie was outfitted with all the necessary towels, dishes, and supplies, and my father was convinced I knew how to operate all the different knobs and understood all the safety regulations ("Be sure to close the propane valve before driving!"), I hugged my folks goodbye at the airport and they flew back to Iowa.

Before they left, they were rather vocal about their concern about Roxie being able to complete the entire month-long trip, so I decided to heed their advice. I scheduled the itinerary with some cushion days to make up for any time we would spend in repair shops across the country, and bought RV tow insurance to cover any unexpected breakdowns. I actually shared my parents' concern a bit, since Roxie wasn't exactly a spring chicken, but at this point, I had no choice but to forge ahead and hope for the best, feeling confident that somehow I'd pull through.

A couple of days later, I had completed all the pre-trip preparations. In the wee hours of the morning on September 22, 2004, I finally dropped off to sleep for my last night at home. The past few weeks had been so hectic that I hardly knew if I was coming or going half the time. It was completely impossible to imagine that this crazy idea was actually going to become reality in mere hours. How I slept, I'll never know, but before I knew it, my alarm had gone off, Judy was in Roxie riding shotgun, and we were on the road to New London, CT, to catch the 12:23 p.m. ferry to Long Island.

I've never traveled over water much. I guess growing up in landlocked states sort of limits how much water travel is necessary, so I've never really gotten comfortable with it. Not only do I have an irrational fear of deep water (I almost drowned in a campground swimming pool when I was seven, and have yet to get over the experience), but I am also very susceptible to motion sickness on water for some reason. I never get air- or carsick, but seasickness is pretty much guaranteed. As a result, if I can get from point A to point B by air or land, I usually opt for one of those choices rather than cross water. Since I was anxious to get settled into the Long Island campground as quickly as possible so I could get a good night's rest before the journey officially started from Sag Harbor, I made the unique decision to risk the one-hour water crossing rather than take a chance on spending half a dozen hours battling New York traffic. So, a tad sleep-deprived and nervous, I found myself driving Roxie into the lower level of the ferry that morning.

Judy stayed below deck in Roxie while I went upstairs to settle in for the ride. It was a glorious morning. The sun was shining brightly on the water, and the clouds were just lazily drifting across the sky. The wind was fresh with the smell of salt water, and the sea was calm. After about 15 minutes, I found myself loosening my grip on my chair and actually starting to enjoy the sensation of the moment. It was all happening. I was starting the adventure of my life, and I was stunned to think that against all odds, I had somehow ended up here—crossing Long Island Sound on a beautiful day, with no idea of what the next month would bring. I only knew that by the time I returned home, I would be a bit poorer, the weather would be a lot colder, and with any luck, I might be a tad wiser. It was exhilarating!

Too soon, it seemed, the idyllic trip was over. I went back downstairs to the RV and found Judy sleeping in the breakfast nook that had quickly become her favorite spot. She woke up when I arrived, and immediately hopped into the driver's seat as she always does when we go anywhere. I can't figure out why she does that. She's nowhere near old enough for a learning permit, let alone a license.

"That's my seat," I reminded her as I stood in the space between the two seats.

She showed me her teeth in an evil grin, established her butt even more solidly onto the seat, lifted her right front leg and leaned onto the steering wheel so I could pet her tummy. I started laughing at her obvious attempts at charm, and as soon as she heard my chuckle, she sneezed twice. Knowing I'd been bested, I rubbed her belly briskly and then tapped her on the rump with my other hand.

"OK. You're done. Get over."

Once Judy realized she'd won, she suddenly had no desire to stay in the seat, so she hopped onto the floor, and then into the passenger seat and eagerly looked out the window at all the other passengers who were getting into their cars. Her one perkable ear perked up as she spotted a very happy-looking lab in another car, and in an instant, I was forgotten. All that existed in the world was that black dog, and Judy's need to dominate it.

I heard the beginnings of an imminent bloodcurdling howl start to gurgle deep within my loveable fluffbag of a travel companion. Within a second, the guttural sounds were spewing out of her saliva-dripping bared mouth in a screeching bark as she smashed her face repeatedly against the window in an attempt to leap through the glass, across two cars, and into the backseat of the green Toyota Camry that housed the happy-go-lucky pup that was the target of Judy's wrath.

As usual, I was mortified.

I tried to distract her with loud verbal scolding, attempted to physically pull her away from the window, and even tried to bribe her with food, but as history has taught me, Judy had gone over to her dark side, and there was nothing that would sway her from her goal until the offending creature was out of sight and smell.

All I could do was mouth "I'm sorry," to all the people who looked at me in shock and surprise, and hope that the doors would open soon so I could drive away from the floppy dog who was now returning Judy's hostility. I watched with envy as the lab's owner said a stern "No," and the dog quieted down immediately and skulked to the other side of the car. Obviously, they had a sane dog.

Once the dog was out of sight, Judy's eyes finally caught sight of the treat, and she moved back to the breakfast nook to eat it—natch. Finally, the ferry doors opened, and Roxie, Judy, and I drove into the bright sunshine of New York.

I arrived at the Eastern Long Island Kampground in the afternoon. I had hoped to meet the owners since they were very excited about my trip and had even sponsored my first evening, but they were sadly out of town. The employees who were filling in for them were incredibly friendly and helpful, and as I found out, I needed a lot of help.

I had never camped alone before, and it quickly became apparent that I was under prepared. I had a flexible sewer pipe and a high-powered extension cord and I thought I was ready to go. Sadly, I was mistaken. I didn't have the attachment for the power cord to the power box or a "topper" thingy for the sewer pipe, and I was expected to have brought my own hose for the water hookup. Not surprisingly, the campground had a store that was able to provide me with the necessary accoutrements to make my stay as high-tech as possible. They even had an Internet jack located in the back of the store. They were very patient with my ignorance and one fellow spent the better part of an hour walking me through everything.

As I left the store when it closed at 4:00 p.m., after unsuccessfully attempting to get online with my dial-up connection (a scenario that was to become very familiar), I ran into a helpful and friendly campground worker with a golf cart.

"Want a ride?" he asked.

"Sure! Just let me grab all my stuff," I said.

As I struggled with my gear, he turned to speak to a man in his 50s who was idling in a red Cadillac next to the golf cart. The gentleman in the car was saying, "I don't think I should stay here next year. I mean, where are all the single women?"

On impulse, I immediately raised my hand, and said, "Right here."

The poor guy looked at me with a completely horrified expression. My campground guy also looked pleasantly shocked. I felt my face turn crimson, and started laughing nervously as I tend to do when my big mouth says things that make situations uncomfortable. I can never seem to stop myself from going for the joke without pondering the consequences. I mean, did I really want these guys to know that I was available...and alone...in an RV...all night...just over there? It was definitely too late now, I guess.

"Weeeeell," the campground guy began, "glad you're staying with us. See, Bob? This is a great place to meet single women."

Poor Bob. He looked as embarrassed as it is possible for a guy in a Caddy to look, and I felt bad that I inadvertently humiliated him simply for a cheap joke. After all, he was probably married and was just shooting the crap with an old buddy. Then again, I thought, if that's the case, it serves him right for disrespecting his wife in that manner, and to be honest with myself, it was a damn hilarious moment and I would have hated myself for not taking it.

"Ha ha ha," I continued to laugh as I climbed into the golf cart and busied myself with my computer so I wouldn't have to make eye contact with either of them.

Bob made a hasty exit, and I can't say I blamed him.

Finally safely back at the campsite, I sat at the picnic table and tied Judy's 40-foot lead around a lovely tree while she and I ate dinner. I tried to take notes on what had happened so far, and what I was planning on doing next, and even made a few phone calls out of sheer loneliness and fear.

Yes, fear had set in finally. The "big picture" is such a demon to me. When I'm starting a project of any sort, be it weeding the yard, tackling a large load of laundry, or driving across the entire United States, I try to escape the "big picture" and focus on the details, but it's always there, lurking behind the immediate stimuli just waiting to pop into my head at my most vulnerable moment. So often I obsess over big picture fears and get so paralyzed at the magnitude of the project that I shut down and just want to throw in the towel. That night, sitting under the tree in the twilight, thoughts of how much land I had to cover before I would be home again kept popping up. I tried to focus instead on the truism that every journey begins with a single step—and is in fact a summation of many, many more steps, not an entity unto itself—yet that was nearly impossible. All I could think about was that I was at the beginning of the biggest challenge of my life, and I was terrified.

Ironically, I heard that Steinbeck had a similar problem, and I read a book called *The East of Eden Letters*—a diary of sorts that he kept while he was writing that book. He said if he focused on the book rather than the writing, he could never get started, so his publisher gave him a large ledger. On the left side, he wrote letters to his publisher every day—a daily warm-up so to speak. On the right side, he wrote *East of Eden*. He started each day without the goal of writing a book, focusing instead on writing a personal letter. Once he got in the groove, the book eventually developed on its own, and quite honestly, I think he did a pretty good job with that one.

That night I miraculously finally got the "big picture" out of my head. It happened when the sun set and the stars came out. Having grown up on the Great Plains, I miss the immenseness of the sky in its uncluttered landscape. Granted, having the ocean within minutes of my house is a good trade-off, but there are times I feel I'm short-changing myself. This night was one of them. Even though I don't live in a big city, my Connecticut town is still pretty well lit, and what stars do come through are hidden behind all the trees and hills in my neighborhood, so I was unprepared for the brilliance and magnitude of eastern Long Island stars. Millions of stars started peeking through the black (and I mean black) sky, and the moon was brighter than I could remember.

It reminded me of lying on the grass in my backyard in Nebraska when as a kid I tried to count all the stars I could see while fireflies dotted the far end of the yard. Nature always seemed to be so much more a part of day-to-day life then. I guess that's the choice you make when you leave the country for the city. You give up the fireflies for accessibility to ethnic restaurants. Usually, I'm quite happy with my choice to be able to get Middle Eastern food in the middle of the night over seeing millions instead of thousands of stars on clear nights, but boy, that first night on Long Island sure reminded me of what price I've paid for 24-hour falafel.

Judy and I sat there under the twinkling lights, and I was amazed that I had ever had any doubts whatsoever about what I was doing. I couldn't believe that I was lucky enough to be spending at least three more weeks like this, sitting in a chair under the stars with nothing on the agenda but to continue onward to another, new place, where I could once again sit on a chair under the stars and ponder the wonder of it all. I slept well.

PART TWO: THE JOURNEY

Long Island, New York, to Hatfield, Massachusetts
Thursday, September 23, 2004

I was up with the birds. I brewed coffee on my stove, ate some break-fast, and took a wonderfully warm shower in the clean facilities at the campground. By 8:30 a.m. I was at the ferry dock waiting to board the 9:35 ferry back to Connecticut. This morning was the 44th anniversary of the start of Steinbeck's trip, and leaving Sag Harbor put me finally on the "official" trip. New Hampshire was my goal for the day, and with such an early start, I was hoping to arrive early enough to have time to cook a fabulous dinner and maybe even add an entry or two to the blog that I had started a few weeks before the trip.

At the ferry dock, I was directed to park Roxie at the front of a line of cars. After a few minutes, more cars filled in behind and alongside us, and I noticed an antique car parked outside my driver's side window. In-trigued, I got out to look at the pristine vehicle up close. As I walked out the passenger door, I was startled by another antique car parked on that side. Behind it was another, and another, and as I walked around the RV, I noticed that we were completely surrounded by six or seven Model A Fords! They were such beautiful cars. I found out they were on their way to a Model A rally in Massachusetts that weekend. How very cool.

The ferry ride was rather uneventful (trip number two with no seasick-ness!) and as we approached New London Navy Yard, I started scanning the waters for a submarine. In *Travels with Charley*, Steinbeck had men-tioned talking to a sailor on his ferry trip. In the book, he was very clear about how strongly he felt about submarines and how they signified the power of war and death. I'd never seen a submarine, and quite honestly, wondered if I would be able to, since they're usually underwater. As the ferry approached the naval shipyard, I was able to finally see a submarine that was partially out of the water. It was apparently being worked on, and it didn't raise any feelings of awe, dread, or really anything in me. In fact, it was a bit of a letdown. I was expecting a much stronger reaction to seeing such a massive weapon of destruction. On that bright and beautiful, sunshiny morning, I took a moment to wonder—if I had viewed my first submarine in 1960 during the Cold War, would I have shared Steinbeck's feelings? Or would I have echoed the views of the sailor John Steinbeck met on the his ferry journey? That working on a submarine was simply a good job with a future? It's hard to say. What struck me most was the fact that now it seemed like such a nonissue. Ironically, and thankfully, after all the decades of propaganda and fear, somehow the "inevitable" global nuclear war simply never happened. It almost seems cartoonish now to think of the hysteria (real and imagined) of the Cold War, but it's only been two decades since it ended. Speaking as a person who grew up diving under school desks during nuclear attack drills, and having "Nuclear Fallout Shelter" signs permanently affixed to her childhood church, I can't help but wonder if people will ever feel this same way about the threat of terrorism that currently hangs over our heads? I suppose they will, eventually. At least I hope so.

The ferry docked, and we waved goodbye to the Model A Fords. I got a bit lost in New London looking for the highway, yet soon we were tooling along Highway 395 towards Norwich. I started to relax. I was finally in my element. A girl, a dog, and an RV. It was a beautiful day. The sun was shining and I was so happy to be over the past week's anxiety. All that pre-planning craziness was behind me. Ahead of me was the unknown. I had a roof over my head, food in the fridge, and lots of road to travel. I found myself laughing and enjoying the pleasure of it all.

At Norwich, I turned onto Highway 2 to catch up with Steinbeck's route. He had gone through Deerfield, Massachusetts, to see his son at school, so I needed to hook up with Highway 91 at Hartford. At Hartford, I turned north and continued on into Massachusetts.

Massachusetts was beautiful, although I was hoping to see more fall foliage than I did. Everything was still pretty green at that time of year, but I was certain that once I reached upper Maine, I would definitely see some color.

Just before Deerfield, I detoured from the Interstate and drove down Highway 5. Since this was undoubtedly the route Steinbeck had taken (Highway 91 wasn't in existence in 1960), I felt it was necessary to approach his first real stop from the same road he did. It was lovely.

Deerfield is quite possibly one of the most beautiful little towns ever. No doubt this is due to the presence of the prestigious Deerfield Academy and Historic Deerfield, Inc., and I'm sure they have a lot to say about the town staying as beautiful as it can be. I drove around the historic section a bit, and took some pictures, but I didn't dawdle long. I was anxious to make New Hampshire by dark, if possible.

Roxie was purring like a kitten. I had fueled up several miles back, and we had been getting better than expected gas mileage—around 10 mpg. When we started seeing signs for Vermont, I started to get excited. Our third state already! How much fun was this? Then, just as I rounded a corner before exit 26 into Bernardston, Roxie started making a very strange noise.

Thmpthmpthmpthmpthmp...Roxie's engine was making a nasty fluttering sound. I eased up off the gas and looked for an exit ramp. The oil pressure gauge was pegged to the left.

"No! No, no, no, no, no!!!" I cried, as I realized that something was dreadfully wrong.

I knew enough about engines to know that I really shouldn't continue to drive, but I didn't have any desire to spend my first night on the road, actually on the road. Luckily, about a quarter of a mile down the road was the exit to Bernardston, and I opted to take it, as Roxie quickly lost power.

I shifted into neutral to spare any unnecessary strain on the engine, and luckily managed to ease up the exit ramp. At the top was a fire station with a very large circular driveway in front that I fortunately managed to coast into under sheer momentum. I said a silent prayer for small favors. At least I wouldn't be stranded in a lane of traffic somewhere. I hit the brakes and came to a complete stop, but Roxie wasn't well. Her engine was making extremely unpleasant sounds, so as soon as I stopped I turned the key to off.

At that very instant, a loud BANG sounded under the hood.

"What the heck was that?!" I exclaimed. I had never heard a vehicle sound like a shotgun went off under the hood before.

Steam poured out of the hood from any point of exit it could find.

"$#&%!" I swore, and swore again, as I jumped out of the cab and cautiously lifted the hood.

My worst fears were realized. Smoke was pouring out of the pipe where one normally adds oil. I knew that wasn't good. I got a sick feeling in my stomach. Then I remembered... I had RV tow insurance! Sure. They could tow me to a dealership, the problem would be fixed, and I could be back on the road tomorrow! Jumping deeper into the oh-so-comfortable world of denial, I thought even though it was late afternoon, maybe there was a dealer nearby that had a mechanic on duty until 9:00 p.m. or so. Maybe I could even get back on the road again tonight? Heck, once they learn what an amazing trip I was taking, maybe they'd even give me a discount or something! Granted, I wouldn't get my relaxing dinner at the campground tonight, but hey, there's always tomorrow night in Maine. So, with a calm sense of optimistic delusion, I pulled out my cell phone, found that I had local coverage (I considered it a good omen), and dialed the emergency 800 number to the RV cavalry.

"How long?" I asked incredulously.

"They'll be there within an hour or two," the cheery voice repeated.

My stomach suddenly didn't feel very good. How the heck was I going to keep on schedule if my first night on the road was going to be spent at an RV dealership? By the time the RV cavalry arrived, would there even be anyone at the dealership, or would it be closed? Would the tow truck be willing to then drive me to a motel, or was I going to be stranded at a deserted car lot in the middle of God-knows-where? Oh, it was all too awful to comprehend.

This was definitely not how things were supposed to be going. Roxie wasn't supposed to break down at all until we at least got out of New England. I had always had imagined us broken down at some mechanic's shop at an old dusty garage in the middle of the picturesque Mojave Desert. Judy would be laying in the shade at my feet in front of an old Standard Station with battered siding while I balanced on a rickety chair leaned back on two legs against the garage door with a beat-up cowboy hat tipped down over my eyes while a tanned and fit gas pump jockey wearing a tight white t-shirt and ripped and paint-splattered jeans played lazy blues songs on the harmonica while passing the time waiting for the next dust-covered car to come in for a fill-up and an iced-cold Coca-Cola from the red cooler at the entrance to the station's front door.

"You need a defibrulatorizonicide cap," the scruffy but completely knowledgeable mechanic named Bubba would yell from the shop.

I'd stick out my bottom lip and take on a squinting air of cautious consideration.

"So…how much do you reckon this is going to set me back?" I'd inquire before spitting a sunflower seed shell on the ground.

"Well, it must be your lucky day. A busload of European tourists broke down here last week, and sold me their vehicle for parts. It's pretty amazing that their 2002 Bluebird bus uses the same engine as your 1978 Chevy. Boy, I'd hate to be you if the situation was different. I figure you should get out of here for around $20 or so, depending on how much of that Coca-Cola you plan on drinkin'. I should have her ready for the road in about five minutes—give or take a minute."

"Well, I'd best be getting' on, then." I'd kick myself off the wall, stand up, and stretch. Judy would follow my initiative and shake the red dust out of her fur. I'd saunter into the store to josh with the locals for the next few minutes, stock up on beef jerky and more sunflower seeds, and grab yet another Coke on my way out the door. Fifteen minutes later, we'd be tooling back down the road watching the sunset over the multi-colored vistas on the horizon while listening to a mariachi tune wafting through on the scratchy AM radio.

Instead, my first breakdown came in a fire station parking lot just shy of Vermont in the rapidly depleting sunlight of my first day on the road.

I tried to pass the next couple of hours by calling relatives and friends for support, reading a bit, and petting Judy, yet all the while I was unnerved by the whole adventure. After all, this was merely a beginning taste of what I might expect over the next few weeks. It was an expected part of the journey; I had just not expected it so soon. "So what?" I thought. "So I'm not in my fantasy breakdown situation. This is reality and this is all just part of the adventure." At times I even convinced myself that I was glad this had happened. At least now I felt like I wasn't in control of everything and the adventure had officially started. After all, wasn't this part of why I wanted to take this trip? To get myself out of my comfort zone and to experience the unexpected? Darn tootin' it was.

After about an hour and a half, the tow truck arrived. The driver was a very enthusiastic young man who taught me a lot about tow-truck driving. He owned the company with his father, and I'd be willing to bet I've never met a man who was more satisfied with his profession—ever. He told me they had a couple of trucks and work was good, and he was quite possibly one of the happiest people I've ever met in my life. He had a good job that made him happy, a good home that was secure, and he seemed to just ooze contentment and joy. Here was a man in his late 20s who was so satisfied with life that his only goals were to continue expanding on what he already had. He thought they might get another truck in a year or so, and he thought he might get a bigger house when he got married, but he truly had no complaints. I was completely enraptured and envious. Since I had brought a video camera along to document my trip, I asked if I could film him telling his story, and he blushed a bit and politely declined, saying he wasn't movie material. I think he was highly mistaken about that. I don't think I've ever met anyone who exuded happiness and calm to the degree that this man did. I just know that if I thought driving a tow truck in northern Massachusetts could make me even half as happy as that man was, I'd leave tomorrow. How I wish it could.

About this time, he had disengaged something under the RV that he needed to disengage in order to hoist Roxie onto the tow truck, and we had climbed into the cab to drive to the RV dealership, when he said, "I'm supposed to take you to an RV dealership in Hatfield."

"What?!" I exclaimed with alarm. "That's back toward Northampton!" I was completely unprepared for this. I didn't want to go backwards. I wanted to go forward—into Vermont—which was just a handful of miles away to the north.

"Yeah, but I'm supposed to take you to the nearest dealership, and that's the closest."

"Will they at least be open?" I asked.

"I don't know," he replied.

"If they're not, are you just going to leave me in an abandoned parking lot?" I was starting to panic a titch.

"Maybe," he said as his bright smile dimmed just a bit. "Let's see what we can do."

He drove that tow truck as quickly as was safe, and just a bit before 6:00 p.m., we pulled into the brightly lit dealership that was thankfully still open. The owner came out, heard my story, and graciously offered to hook us up with water and electricity in the gated back lot. I was completely relieved to know that in the morning, there was going to be a mechanic reporting to work promptly at 8:00 a.m., and Roxie would be the first thing on his schedule. I felt that once again, things were going to be OK. The mechanic would look at Roxie, figure out what was wrong, hopefully fix it in a couple of hours, and it was possible that I could be back on the road by late morning! Mostly, I was happy to know that people knew where I was and that I would be taken care of as quickly as possible. For the moment, I might have been in the middle of nowhere, but I wasn't alone.

After setting Roxie up for the night, the owner was on his way home, and since I had had a stressful day, I asked him if he could tell me where I might be able to get some beer in the neighborhood. He generously drove me down the road to a liquor store, and bade me good night. After purchasing a six-pack of ale, I began the walk back to the dealership.

The night was beautiful. The sun was setting and the stars were coming out. It wasn't dark enough yet to need a flashlight, and as I walked across ditches and yards along Highway 5, I started to relax again. I took the time to look at the houses and fields that I was passing and was struck by the difference between New England farms and the Midwestern ones of my childhood. The fields in Massachusetts are much, much smaller, but they possess a calmness and charm that doesn't exist in the expansive farms of the heartland. There were highway stands selling corn and apples, and some of the houses offered "pick your own" berries. I breathed in the warm and clear night air and felt the stresses of the past few weeks ease off of my shoulders. I lifted my gaze into the deepening twilight and saw a hot air balloon floating above me several hundred feet up, lazily drifting into the sunset. For a moment, life was perfect.

I shifted the increasingly heavy six-pack to my other arm and started to realize that I had been walking for quite a while. I checked my watch. It had been over 20 minutes since I left the liquor store, and I didn't think I was anywhere near the dealership yet. Just how far had we driven? I couldn't remember, but it only seemed to have taken about five minutes, so I figured it wasn't that far.

Twenty minutes later, I was still walking, and my mood had shifted from bliss to bunk. Road travel sucked. This whole trip sucked. Why the heck was I cursed with the need to do crazy things like this? Why couldn't I be happy driving a tow truck, too? Who were the people in the balloon, all ooing and ahhing as they floated above me watching the pretty sunset? Why couldn't I be them? And how the #*!$ much farther was this place?

Approximately 50 minutes after leaving the store, I finally reached the RV dealership. I was hot, sweaty, cranky, and amazed at exactly how far I am apparently willing to walk for a beer. But at least I was back home in Roxie again. Judy had been sleeping, but she woke up when I arrived. I got us both dinner, and then we took a quick walk around the RV lot. When we returned, she jumped onto her spot at the breakfast nook and lay down with a heavy sigh. I sat down opposite her, opened a beer, and looked at my map of the United States again. My highlighted journey was too enormous to comprehend. It was over 10,000 miles long, passed through 36 states, and touched two oceans. Steinbeck traversed the

North American continent and back in three and a half months. Somehow, God willing, I was going to be doing it in less than a third of that time. Considering that I had already been traveling for approximately 36 hours, but was still less than two hours from home, it was almost impossible to believe I would ever complete the journey in its entirety.

To get my mind off the big picture, I climbed out of the RV, and took another look at the night. The stars were out, but due to the harsh security lights of the dealership lot, I wasn't able to get as close to the sky as I wanted. I went back into Roxie, grabbed another beer and a folding chair, and headed back outside. I went around to the back of Roxie, and climbed the ladder to the roof. Once there, I set up the chair and popped open the second beer. As I sat there under the umbrella of stars, above the parking lot lights, I found that if I squinted, I could almost imagine that I was indeed in a cozy campground in New Hampshire, about to set off in the morning to Deer Isle, Maine, and all the glories it promised. And as much as I didn't want to be stuck in Massachusetts, I was somehow able to absorb the moment and truly appreciate how, as Steinbeck so eloquently noted, "We don't take a trip; a trip takes us."

Hatfield, Massachusetts
Friday, September 24, 2004

I slept fitfully, but woke up hopeful. With any luck, today the mechanic was going to fix Roxie and I would be on my way, only a day behind schedule.

After having my morning coffee and breakfast, it was still too early for anyone to be at work, so Judy and I took a walk around the lot and peeked into the other RVs. My goodness, some of them were big. They were literally buses, and cost hundreds of thousands of dollars. They sure were nice, though. What would it be like to be living in one of these mobile units? Would it be a free existence where you just drift with the weather, or is it terribly limiting due to the sheer size of the vehicles and the amount of maintenance they require? Where do you get a bus serviced, anyway? I don't think my local garage could accommodate something that large.

Then I looked back at Roxie. She looked so small and drab compared to the gleaming behemoths surrounding her. I felt such a wave of affection for her. She might certainly be less shiny than the others, but she was mine.

The mechanic showed up promptly at 8:00 a.m., and immediately took a look at Roxie. By 8:10 a.m., he had determined that she was beyond repair.

What?! How could he decide that so quickly? He couldn't tell me exactly what was wrong without running some tests, and yet he felt there was no need to run any tests because she was obviously done for.

My stomach dropped.

Then my Irish got up.

Just who did this mechanic think he was? I wasn't born yesterday, and he came to this conclusion rather quickly. Was it any coincidence that they just happened to be in the business of selling RVs? I was skeptical to say the least, and I immediately began grilling any mechanic, salesperson, or owner who happened by me as to what they were going to do to help me.

It quickly became obvious that they weren't even going to consider trying to fix Roxie. After all, they were a dealership—not a repair shop. Since I was miles from anywhere, and had no idea where I might find someone to take an unbiased look at her, not to mention I had a definite time limit, I had no choice but to see what other options might be available to me. After all, they were a dealership. Maybe they could work out some sort of arrangement for a vehicle newer than Roxie, and I could continue my trip in a more reliable method of transportation. It seemed like a practical idea, but it was heartbreaking. I had gotten so attached to Roxie in the past week that to lose her so soon seemed unfair. Just a few days ago, my dad and I had ripped out the shag carpeting and put in a lovely new floor. The shower curtain, the garbage cans, the hangers in the closet, the mattress cover, even the blind-spot side mirrors were all new and hardly broken in. I hadn't even had the opportunity to use the shower yet.

Then again, what were my options? Just throw in the towel and go home? How would I ever be able to face all those people who were counting on me? Surely there had to be a way to continue onward. I hadn't spent this much time, effort, and money to give up now.

Finally after many hours of filling out paperwork, getting declined by finance companies, and drinking as much free coffee as I could, things still weren't looking very good. It seems getting financing for an RV is a little more complicated than getting, say, a car loan or a mortgage. The financing organizations apparently want more money down, better credit scores, and more than the pint of blood I was willing to give for a new vehicle. Once it became clear that I wasn't able to qualify for a loan, the attitude of the folks at the dealership cooled toward me drastically. Within minutes, I went from being their top priority to being ignored completely. They even towed Roxie from the gated area behind the building to the front public parking lot and pretended I didn't exist. I found myself sitting in the parking lot completely stranded.

What was I to do now? The only people nearby couldn't have cared less what I did or didn't do, so I snuck back inside, stole a phone book, and started looking for other dealerships in the area who might be more helpful. One dealership, Longview RV in Northampton, was just a couple of miles down the road and the salesperson even offered to come get me so I could see what they had to offer. I locked Judy in Roxie, snuck across the parking lot, and waited behind a bunch of bushes a couple dozen yards down the road, where the Longview salesperson asked me to meet her. She didn't want to be seen "stealing" a customer from the competitors. It felt so very clandestine and sneaky, and added a bit of melodrama to the otherwise depressing and hopeless day. Then again, if the first dealership had any amount of customer service common sense, they would have done what they could to see that I got on my way—even if it meant calling the other dealership down the road—so I felt if they lost a customer, it's because they earned it.

Upon arriving at Longview, I immediately felt much better. The staff was actually concerned with my plight, and wanted to do what they could to help me out. They would have their mechanic look at Roxie, and if she wasn't fixable, they had a used vehicle that would meet my needs. They were willing to offer me the same value for trade-in on Roxie that I had originally paid for her, and no matter what, they felt they could have me on the road again by morning. Hurrah! I was back on schedule.

So, I snuck back to the first dealer, and when no one was watching, fired up Roxie (who sounded horrible), and drove the few miles back to Longview RV. When I arrived, smoke was pouring out of the engine once again. The friendly and compassionate folks helped me hook up to their water and electricity for the night, and with cheery smiles and optimism, pointed me in the direction of a highly recommended BBQ restaurant about a quarter of a mile away—just past the liquor store that I had been to the night before. I was so grateful I almost cried.

In *Travels with Charley*, Steinbeck mentioned a powerful sermon he heard in a Vermont church. I, too, had been planning on attending a church in New England to see if there were still any fire-and-brimstone preachers around looking to knock some common sense back into this doomed sinner. However, my first visit to a church on this journey ended up being not only amazingly eye-opening, but also mouth-watering.

Holy Smokes BBQ & Whole Hog House restaurant in West Hatfield, Massachusetts, was located in a steepled, deconsecrated Lutheran church building that was built in 1889, and moved to its 2004 location in 1948. Steinbeck undoubtedly drove right past it in 1960 when it was still an operating place of worship. In 2004, however, it was home to the most amazing BBQ I've had north of the Mason-Dixon line.

After walking the few hundred yards to the church from the RV dealership, I found that the restaurant was rather popular, even though it had only been open for a few months. There was a line out the front door, and the wait list for a "pew" was almost an hour. (The original cushioned pews from the church are the seats at the tables.) There was also a large reservation for a wedding rehearsal dinner, so there were even fewer available tables than usual. Since I had nowhere else to go, I moved back outside to wait in the warm twilight with the rest of the crowd.

Suddenly, several motorcycles appeared. Eight of the most intimidating women I've ever seen parked their bikes in a row, and filed onto the sidewalk. They were tattooed, pierced, buff, and leather-clad specimens of the female gender, and they were laughing and full of good cheer. The group was shown to the reserved table for the wedding dinner. At that moment, I remembered that on May 17, 2004, Massachusetts had passed the first same-sex marriage law in the country. The women were lesbians celebrating upcoming nuptials. It was all so perfect. I couldn't think of a more shocking contrast to Steinbeck's more traditional New England church experience.

Just when I thought it couldn't get any better, one of the women laughed and loudly declared, "I can't believe I'm doing this on Yom Kippur!" A Jewish lesbian was attending her friends' same-sex wedding rehearsal dinner at a restaurant in a deconsecrated Protestant church that specialized in BBQ pork on one of the High Holy Days.

My grin practically split my head open. I simply couldn't make this stuff up.

Hatfield, Massachusetts, to Lancaster, New Hampshire
Saturday, September 25, 2004

I woke up Saturday morning feeling numb. Maybe it was all the hot BBQ from the night before, but I hardly slept a wink. Although there was a slim chance that I would be able to get into a new RV that day, I wasn't feeling too hopeful about it. It was starting to seem like I would be stuck in Massachusetts forever.

It was Saturday, and there wouldn't be any mechanics on duty until Monday. I knew I couldn't wait that long to see what was really wrong with Roxie, so the only alternative that I felt was available to me was to find financing for a used vehicle on the lot. If that didn't work, well, I felt I was out of options, and would have to find a way to get back home.

While I was waiting to hear from the banks, a friendly fellow wearing a garish red, white, and blue tie dropped by the dealership and started chatting. His name was Bill Volk, and it turned out that he was the balloonist that I had seen flying the night before. He had some photos of some local "crop art"—pictures that are "drawn" in cornfields by cutting down the tall cornstalks, and are only visible from the sky. I was amazed. They were like fancy UFO crop circles, except these were portraits of George W. Bush, scarecrows, and all sorts of other complicated images. He was a warm and friendly bright spot in my otherwise emotionally cloudy day. He even gave me a CD of ballooning images and mentioned that the Albuquerque Ballooning Festival would be happening around the time that I should be in New Mexico.

That is, I thought, if I ever get to New Mexico.

Just before noon, I was summoned into the owner's office and was informed that there wasn't anything they could do for me. They couldn't find financing for me, they didn't have any sort of rental program, and they weren't able to work out any sort of sponsorship of my trip. I was disappointed, but not terribly surprised. At least they tried. In sharp contrast to the other dealership, everyone at Longview was terribly sad for me. They let me hang out as long as I wanted, and let me know they'd do whatever they could to help me. I felt that these people wanted me to succeed on this trip as much for their own sake as for mine.

After receiving this news, I wandered out into the RV lot and called my parents with the bad news. As soon as I heard the disappointment in my mother's voice, I completely lost it and broke down in tears. How could it all be happening like this? Even the comforting words of, "At least you tried. Maybe you can try again next year?" from my mother didn't ease the pain and anger I was feeling. A year and a half of my life had gone into the planning and anticipation of this trip, and it ended a mere 90 miles north of where I started.

Once the painful crying jag was over, I finally allowed myself to think about quitting. I was ready to give up. I had tried and failed. It wasn't so bad to admit to; after all, better people than I have done the same. Abraham Lincoln's many failures came to mind, and look at what he eventually accomplished. Quitting wasn't the ideal situation, but then again, I still had almost a month off of work, and several thousand dollars left in the bank. I could cut my losses, take a vacation somewhere else, and maybe try this again in another year (although that seemed almost too painful to consider at the moment.)

Once I shifted my thinking to going back instead of forward, new problems came to light. Exactly how was I going to get back home? After all, it wasn't possible to tow Roxie that far, but I had so much stuff (dishes, towels, the new garbage can, etc.) that I needed to transport back to Connecticut. I thought about renting a van, but that, too, would be extremely expensive, and I didn't even know if there was a van available for rent in the area. Then, like a lightning bolt, it hit me. Why couldn't I buy a van? After all, my credit might have been too bad to buy an RV, but it wasn't too bad to buy a car.

In that instant, I realized it wasn't over yet. I yelled out a rousing "YES!" and literally ran back into the dealership. When I burst into the building, the staff looked up in shock, until I eagerly asked if anyone knew of a used car lot where I could buy a van. Faces lit up and beamed! People came running out of their offices to lend a hand. One salesman grabbed the phone and called a friend of his who was a salesman at a car lot in Brattleboro, Vermont. After a quick chat on the phone, and the joyous guarantee that there was indeed a used van on the lot that I could afford, I sat back to wait for the salesman to run my credit check.

Everyone in the office was laughing—especially me. I realized that it wasn't over until it's over, and it now looked like the adventure might just be beginning. Life truly can turn on a dime.

A few minutes later, I got the call that I had been approved for a loan, and that my new best buddy, Al Germain from the Auto Mall in Brattleboro, Vermont, was driving the soon-to-be-mine 2002 GMC Savana cargo van down to Northampton to pick up me, Judy, and Roxie, and he'd be there in about an hour.

It was the longest hour I've ever had to wait.

"Roxie II" appeared on the horizon just over an hour later. She was beautiful.

And new.

And large.

And blue.

She was an extended-length cargo van, and had a big equipment rack on the roof. Inside, she was outfitted with lots of industrial shelving to hold all of my many belongings and a lockable metal door that separated the cab from the storage area. She had air-conditioning, cruise control, and cup holders. She was perfect, and she was mine.

Al decided it would be best for me to follow him in Roxie II, while he drove Roxie back to Brattleboro, since she was in such precarious shape. That was fine with me because I wanted to give the van a test drive anyway. We started slowly driving up Highway 5.

A couple of miles up the road, however, Roxie literally exploded. It was like a bomb had gone off under the RV. Large quantities of stuff that looked like large pieces of paper or cardboard blew out the exhaust, and Al swerved a bit from the blast. He immediately lost power and pulled over to what little shoulder there was on the highway. My heart sank again. What now?

By the time I had pulled over with the van, Al was already deep underneath the hood of Roxie surveying the damage. Apparently, she had thrown a rod straight through the engine. She wasn't going anywhere.

Al, being a man of resources and spunk, seemed unfazed by the whole thing.

"Boy! That rod shot straight through the engine! I'm lucky it didn't fly through the dashboard and impale me," he chuckled. "No matter. I'll just have them bring the tow truck down and we'll haul it up to my property in northern Vermont. I guess that means that we'd better move your stuff to the van now."

Huh? He still wanted the vehicle? There weren't going to be any "new negotiations" on the trade-in value? Everything was just this easy? Well, I thought, I guess it's about time something good happened on this trip.

So, after dodging traffic as we moved absolutely everything from inside Roxie to Roxie II, we zipped up the highway and after two days, finally crossed that last handful of Massachusetts' miles and arrived in Vermont at long last.

* * * * *

"Say cheese!" Al chirped as he took a picture of Judy and me in front of Roxie II. It was a few hours later, we had finally completed all the paperwork, and we were just about to shove off towards New Hampshire for the night. I smiled, but I felt positively drained, sad, and was having major buyer's remorse. Sure, Roxie II was a fine specimen of an automobile, but seeing the original Roxie on that tow truck, knowing I might never see her again, was just too painful. It was like a beloved pet had died.

I waved goodbye to Al and the rest of the friendly folks at the Auto Mall, and headed north as the sun was setting. It was odd getting used to the ease of the drive at first. Roxie had been terribly bumpy, everything rattled, and I couldn't go faster than about 60 mph without the engine straining, while Roxie II just purred along effortlessly no matter how fast I tried to push her. For the first time since I started, I felt confident that I would be able to complete the trip. Although I might have been less sentimentally attached to the van, I was actually rather relieved to be rid of the constant anxiety of potential breakdowns of the RV. Mostly, though, I was simply glad to be back on the road and heading forward once again.

We spent that night in a campground near Lancaster, New Hampshire. It was late when we arrived, and since I didn't have a place to sleep anymore, we rented a cabin for the evening. Although I was exhausted upon arriving, I tried to get some quick writing done before dozing off. It had certainly been a stressful past few days, but at that moment, as I looked around the knotty pine walls of the cabin and saw Judy lying peacefully on her side in a deep sleep, I felt content.

Lancaster, New Hampshire, to Deer Isle, Maine
Sunday, September 26, 2004

Sunday morning dawned bright and clear. I stepped out of the cabin and was blinded by the brilliance of the White Mountains that served as a backdrop to the campsite. I felt like I was in a living and breathing postcard. Who knew nature could sneak up on you like that?

After a leisurely shower in the campground's very nice facilities, I once again loaded up the van and hit the road. Today we were finally going to make it to the mystical Deer Isle, Maine.

Before we got to Maine, though, there was one place I wanted to see. Steinbeck had mentioned a small motel just outside Lancaster near the Connecticut River where he pulled up to sleep for the night. Upon arriving, he found that though the motel and its café were by all appearances open, there wasn't a soul around. He waited and waited, and finally just spent the night in Rocinante, but by the next morning no one had appeared, and around 9:30 a.m., he left, feeling rather disturbed by it all.

I approached the metal bridge over the Connecticut River. There was no such motel, only an ordinary chain gas station and convenience store on one side of the road, and a field on the other. I have to admit that this was the first (but not the last) time that I would feel somewhat cheated. I knew when I began this journey that a lot of what Steinbeck described wouldn't actually be there anymore. And yet, I guess deep down I hoped that maybe a small business like the motel might have survived. After all, we were very near Mount Washington, and the tourists still flowed into the White Mountains every year, so why wouldn't a small motel be able to continue to thrive? By the looks of the gas station, business was good.

Most likely the owner died and no one in the family wanted to take over the business, so they sold it to a company who tore the buildings down and built a gas station on the property. Then again, Steinbeck had said that he was exhausted from road travel. Since he never actually saw any people there, maybe it was all an hallucination created by his tired mind? Probably not, but I have to admit I like the idea of it being a ghost motel. It's just a much better story than the boring old "progress" explanation.

Mount Washington sure is big. As we got close to the turnoff to Mount Washington, I admit I caught a bit of summit fever. Sure, Steinbeck never mentioned driving to the top, but heck, it was *there*. So, I turned Roxie II down the road and joined the line of fellow mountain climbers as they waited to pay for the opportunity to drive to the highest peak in the northeastern United States.

While we waited, I tried to remember everything I could about the mountain, but all I could remember was that it had the dubious honor of being able to brag of having the worst weather on the planet. The highest wind speed ever recorded was on the top of the mountain, clocked in at an astonishing 231 MPH, so actually, it ain't bragging.

The line moved slowly and I felt myself getting anxious about time. I wanted to get to Deer Isle at a decent hour since I needed to find a place to sleep. I didn't know exactly how many options would be available that time of year to a weary traveler with a dog. Before I left home, I had made arrangements to park the RV at a campground run by the ever-so-friend-ly Captain Bill, but since I no longer had an RV, and I didn't know if he had any cabins (although I hoped so.) I wanted to get there early enough to find alternate accommodations if necessary. More than once I reached for my cell phone to make a call to Captain Bill, but cell reception was zip, as had been the case since I left Massachusetts.

Another 10 or 15 minutes crawled by, and I finally got to the gate.

"Twenty-five dollars, lady," the not-so-cheery gatekeeper said.

"What?! You want me to pay you twenty-five dollars to allow me to drive up this mountain?" I responded in shock. Annual memberships to National Parks are less.

"Yep. Twenty-five dollars."

That cured my summit fever.

I was directed to a well-marked turnaround lane (apparently I wasn't the first to get sticker shock) and returned to my original plan of getting to Maine before dark. I cruised through the remainder of New Hampshire as quickly as I could. Compared to most western states, Maine isn't very big, but it certainly was the biggest state I had tried to cross so far. I knew it would take longer than the hour or so it took to cross the others.

Ah, Maine. The land of cute little houses on cute little roads and bumpy two-lane highways and spotty cell reception. It was a rather uneventful drive across the state. Judy and I only stopped briefly to pick up some road staples like beef jerky and sodas. I was exhausted by the time we reached Bangor and needed to turn south to Deer Isle. Unlike Steinbeck, I didn't get lost once.

Steinbeck started his trip by visiting the home of Eleanor Brace, a friend of his longtime friend and agent, Elizabeth Otis, who stayed on Deer Isle every year. Ms. Otis was so enraptured with the island that she had insisted that he go, and notified Ms. Brace that he would be visiting. Steinbeck felt he had no choice but to oblige. In the end, he too fell under the spell of the isle and even compared it to the mythical Isle of Avalon. I had to see what the fuss was all about.

Prior to leaving, I had tried to locate the address of the home, but had some difficulty. Originally, I was prepared to drive to Deer Isle and ask the locals to point out the place, but then while planning for the trip I was cornered by an enthusiastic coworker.

"You're planning on doing the *Travels with Charley* trip?" she asked.

I told her that that was the plan.

She excitedly told me of the incredibly fortuitous coincidence that not only was she from Maine, but another coworker of ours who was also from Maine actually knew Brenda Gilchrist, the niece of Miss Eleanor Brace, who currently lived in the Deer Isle home.

"Brenda is such a nice person. You have to go see her!" she exclaimed. It seems people's enthusiasm for the Brace/Gilchrist family hasn't changed much in 44 years.

And so, after getting Brenda Gilchrist's address from my colleague, sending her a letter outlining my plan, and receiving a very positive response, I found myself eagerly, but somewhat nervously, preparing for my first real-live interview with a connection to Steinbeck's past.

The whole coast of Maine seemed so odd to me. I was expecting it to be more like Connecticut, where the land ends and the water begins—just like that. However, coastal Maine doesn't really feel like a coast. It feels more like a very large flooded area with individual islands between small strips of water. Each time I went over a bridge, I kept thinking that the other side must be Deer Isle, only to be mistaken. Even after traveling over the large metal arched bridge that Steinbeck mentioned, I thought that surely, the other side must be my destination. Alas, I was wrong. There was still an s-curved bridge that spanned yet another body of water. By this point, I started to believe Steinbeck's comparison to Avalon and that the ever-elusive island could only be reached by those worthy enough. I was pretty sure I wasn't.

Once we got over the low bridge, however, there was a small white building on the right-hand side of the road that had a sign announcing that it was Deer Isle's information building. Near dusk on a Sunday evening, there was no one there, but in front of the building was a small wood and plastic display case that held several copies of a map of the isle and the *Island Guide for Deer Isle and Stonington, Maine*. All for free. How convenient! I located the Old Quarry Adventure Campground, home of the legendary Captain Bill whom I had had several e-mail conversations with, and started off toward Stonington.

In no time at all, Judy and I pulled up to the cute main building of Old Quarry Adventures located on the water at the end of Deer Isle. I noticed that there were RV hookups near the entrance, and once again, my heart panged at the loss of Roxie. I went up to the door, and saw a sign that said, "Back at 6:00," even though the door was wide open. It was nearing 6:00 p.m., so I let myself into the office and started snooping around at the objects for sale while I waited. Not two minutes later, a sprightly and friendly gent walked in the door.

"Are you Captain Bill?" I asked excitedly, never actually having met a captain before.

"Yep."

"I'm Vicki Cain. I e-mailed you about my trip recreating *Travels with Charley*? I know I'm a day late, but our RV died in Massachusetts, and there's no cell reception in the greater part of upper New England, so I wasn't able to call."

"Oh! I was wondering what happened to you. Where's the dog?" He peered over my shoulder and looked out the door toward Roxie II.

In my absence, Judy had decided to hop into the driver's seat and was looking back at him with a big smile on her face and her ear up. Captain Bill saw her and laughed a warm and infectious laugh. I was instantly smitten.

"You know, a couple of years ago, another woman came through here doing this same trip. She said she had read Steinbeck's book and was so impressed with it that she wanted to see everything that he had seen. Apparently, she didn't have a dog, so she bought one for the trip."

My expression must have been one of pure shock.

"She bought a *dog* for the trip? Like it was a tent or something?" I asked incredulously.

"That's what she said. I never heard back from her. I wonder if she ever finished?" he mused.

I was stunned. Why would anyone adopt a dog simply to recreate someone else's life? I had trouble wrapping my brain around the idea.

All my life I've been an advocate for lost animals. My family has always gotten their pets at the Humane Society, a shelter, or from friends who, for whatever reason, couldn't provide for the pet anymore. Even Judy came from the dog pound.

One time, my parents were even part of a "black market" dog adoption outside a Humane Society one cold and rainy night. They had gone to the shelter looking for a small dog to replace the hole in their lives that was created by the deaths of their two geriatric dogs. Alas, the shelter only had larger dogs at that time, so my parents left dejected.

Suddenly, a man appeared from behind a minivan in the parking lot and said, "I understand you're looking for a small dog?"

"Yes, we are, but they didn't have any today," my father replied.

"We have one, if you're interested," the stranger said.

He lifted the tailgate of the minivan, and inside was a small animal carrier with a Cocker Spaniel-mix puppy shivering inside. Above the cage and behind the last seat of the van, five little children with tear-streaked faces looked back at my parents with big, sad eyes.

"You see, she barks a lot and the neighbors have complained, so we need to find her a home."

The kids stared at my parents, and as the two dads talked and my mother petted the dog, a couple of the older kids started looking a little hopeful. As they talked, it became clear that they lived only a few blocks away from my parents, which cheered the children up even more.

Needless to say, my parents couldn't refuse. To this day, my mother says she felt like she was committing some crime by accepting a pet from the back of a van, at night, in the rain, in a shelter's parking lot.

I'm not sure how Steinbeck acquired Charley, but he says, "He was born in Bercy on the outskirts of Paris and trained in France, and while he knows a little poodle-English, he responds quickly onto commands in French. Otherwise he has to translate, and that slows him down." So, it sounds like Charley was more of a *bleu* blood poodle than a shelter dog to me.

I wonder if the dog that was purchased for that woman's trip ended up at a shelter once the journey was over? It baffles and infuriates me how casually people discard domesticated animals, yet it seems to happen quite frequently. Then again, maybe I'm not being fair. It's entirely possible that this woman had always wanted a dog, and Steinbeck's book simply motivated her to finally fulfill her dream. It's quite possible that the two of them are living happily together, thankful that the power of Steinbeck's words brought them together. That's what I choose to believe. I have to.

Once the Captain and I got past the introductions, he informed me that he did not have any cabins, but did offer to let me have a tent for cheap. Considering I was supposed to be meeting Ms. Gilchrist in the morning, I wanted to get a good night's sleep, and since spending a night in a tent didn't seem like the best way to accomplish that, I asked him for a motel referral. He suggested Boyce's Motel in Stonington, and thanks to my new Deer Isle guide, I found their number and called to see if there were any vacancies. Fortunately for us, there were.

The motel was located on Main Street by the harbor. By the time we arrived, checked in, and unloaded the van, it was after dark and I was starving. On this trip I began to realize for the first time, that in many areas of the country, people don't live in a 24-hour world of homogenized chain stores. I was on a small island where people close their businesses and go home for dinner. It was a bit of a shock to think that I might have to go hungry for the evening. I drove up and down Main Street looking for any store or restaurant that might be open past dark, but to no avail. Everything was buttoned up tight and the streets were deserted. Apparently, fishermen go to bed early. I inquired at the motel office for help with finding sustenance, and fortunately for me, there was one (and only one) restaurant still open (until 7:00 p.m.) and it was within walking distance of the motel. It was the Fisherman's Friend restaurant. I was never so thrilled to walk up a steep hill on a deserted road in the dark to a small building with twinkling lights. The food was fabulous.

Deer Isle, Maine, to St. Albans, Vermont
Monday, September 27, 2004

After sleeping like the dead, I woke feeling refreshed and alive. Judy was eager to go out in the morning, so I put the coffee on, grabbed a jacket and her leash, stepped into the day, and immediately froze in my tracks. The view from the stairway of the motel was exquisite. The gray, misty morning fog was drifting lazily across the sun, which was just starting to peek above the horizon. Gulls darted hither and thither across the ocean, which gleamed in the early light like a sheet of gold against the gray backdrop of the sky. The white and gray clapboard buildings of Main Street looked so perfect, that they didn't seem real. It was as if Disney had built this perfect town on this perfect harbor, only it wasn't a facsimile. Everything was real, and it simply took my breath away. For this view on a daily basis, I would happily forgo 24-hour grocery stores and fast food.

The morning activity in Stonington is the opposite of the evening. There were tons of people scurrying about, getting ready for the busy work-day ahead. After her morning constitutional, Judy retired to the back of Roxie II to have her breakfast, and I hit the local restaurant. As with everything else that morning, it was perfect. I had a huge plate of eggs, hash browns, and toast with lots of steaming hot coffee, and paid a very reasonable price for it. I even picked up a local newspaper to see what I'd missed over the past few days.

The headline stated that the *Queen Mary 2* was on her maiden voyage from Europe and was arriving in Bar Harbor that day. I couldn't believe my luck! I decided then and there that after I met with Ms. Gilchrist, I was going to swing up the coast to get a glimpse of the ship. After all, in this day and age of airline travel, it's not everyday an ocean liner makes a maiden voyage, and it's even rarer that it's a sister ship of the only liner I've ever been on, having toured the *Queen Mary* at its dry dock in Long Beach, CA. This was yet another of the happy coincidences that were speckled throughout the trip. I felt like the bad days of the journey were behind me. Things were starting to look up.

With map and detailed directions from Ms. Gilchrist herself in hand, I finally set off to find the legendary residence of her aunt Miss Eleanor Brace. For the first time this trip, I got completely lost. Granted, I was trying to approach the property from the opposite direction as my instructions, but after unsuccessfully trying to locate the turnoff, I found myself back at the information center on the far end of the island. Oops. Gathering my wits, I tried once again from the correct direction, and lo and behold, I drove straight there. It was exactly as it was described in *Travels with Charley.*

According to a short story written by Brenda Gilchrist that was published in the *Eggemoggin Reach Review: An Anthology of Prose and Poetry,* the house "was designed in 1902 by Alexander Wadsworth Longfellow, Henry Wadsworth's nephew, for another uncle of his, James Croswell, also my great-uncle, whose wife, Leta, my great-aunt, left it to her niece, my aunt Eleanor, who left it to me." Of course, Judy and I didn't know any of this at the time of our arrival, but over the next few hours, we were to find out lots of interesting things about Deer Isle, Steinbeck, and Ms. Gilchrist.

We pulled to the side of what I decided must be the garage, or carriage house, or something like that, and heard a small dog barking furiously inside the larger house several dozen yards away. Knowing Judy wouldn't be polite to her canine host, I hurriedly jumped out of the driver's door, and locked the would-be psycho-pooch inside. She immediately jumped into the driver's seat to see where I was going, and I crossed my fingers that the house was just too far away for her to hear, smell, or see the other dog, and therefore she would appear to be a totally normal dog to Ms. Gilchrist.

As I walked down the drive toward the house, the beauty of the spot took me aback. Steinbeck had only commented on the mysteriousness of the isle, and on the ominous and pervasive spirit of evil that surrounded the property—the elusive, but ever-present, just-out-of-sight, George. George was Miss Brace's cat. Apparently, he wasn't exactly the friendliest of felines, and Steinbeck made it clear in no uncertain terms he returned the sentiment. If anyone ever had a doubt as to whether Steinbeck was a dog or a cat person, I think his description of George clears that issue right up.

But back to the beauty. The bright sunlight was filtered through the flickering leaves of the trees high above me, and the ground was comfortably soft and spongy. I could smell the ocean air in the warm breeze, and as I approached the house, the world's most beautiful garden greeted me with flowering, blooming, and climbing flowers and plants that were arranged on trellises and arbors which invited me to walk amongst them for a while. I've never been a gardener, and have never found the time to learn the names of all the plants and flowers that capture my senses, but I've always been lured to the beauty of nature, and this garden was in literal and figurative full-bloom.

The door opened, and a smiling and youthful white-haired woman came out to greet me. She was wearing a pair of comfortable pants, a soft sweater, and sandals with socks. She looked so confident and secure, that I felt a bit self-conscious of my "road clothes"—casual long-sleeved t-shirt and sturdy blue jeans. She was warm and soft-spoken and had a gentleness about her that suggested a profound contentment with life in general. I adored her immediately. My first impression was that Brenda Gilchrist was exactly the sort of person I have always hoped to be one day, but I strongly doubt I'll ever be even close.

She graciously led me around the property and told me stories that her aunt had told her about Steinbeck's visit. She finally led me into the main house, and gave me a tour of the living room.

Exquisite wood paneling lined walls covered with old photographs and maps. A large stone fireplace was at one side of the room, and a small stairway crept up an adjacent wall. The north-facing wall was full of windows that looked out over the water, and there was a door to a screened porch on the far wall. Old couches and striking wood bureaus, tables, and chairs were situated around the room to give one full advantage of the many different views the room offered. It was still furnished with the same furniture and decorations as when her aunt lived there, and probably even her aunt's aunt. That's one thing I have to say for New Englanders. They certainly have more respect for the past than other areas of the country. In fact, I commented that I found it amazing that she never felt the urge to redecorate and make the place more "hers."

"Oh, I could never do that," she said. "I feel like there are too many ghosts in here who would be watching."

Brenda showed me some books she had illustrated and written starring her lovely little corgi, Gabi. Now Gabi was the sort of dog that Judy could aspire to be. She was polite, friendly, and obedient. She also had quite an attitude about her house, and was a little hesitant to let me enter, but once she sniffed me a bit, she realized I was OK, for the moment anyway. I felt privileged to be given such an honor so quickly.

I asked Brenda how she felt things on Deer Isle had changed over the past four decades, since it appeared to me that things were pretty much the same. Even the furniture seemed permanent.

"Well, we managed to avoid a lot of the progress that has gone on in areas like coastal Connecticut and Long Island, but sadly, we've finally been discovered," she said with a heavy voice. "Since the fishing industry has become almost obsolete, we're needing to depend more and more on tourism for support. As a result, people from larger cities are now moving in and driving up the property values so high that people who are born here aren't able to live here."

She gestured across the property toward the quaint guest cottage where John Steinbeck's agent, Elizabeth Otis, had stayed every summer for over 30 years. Elizabeth was the reason Steinbeck visited Deer Isle. She insisted he visit Miss Brace.

"The property just beyond the cottage has been sold, and they're building a large house just over those trees," Brenda said. She looked up at the sky and shook her head. "It's going to feel strange to have people looking into my yard."

As I stood there in the dappled sunlight breathing the fresh air and listening to nothing but the sounds of the trees, birds, and squirrels rustling about their daily lives, I could understand her sadness. If things continued as they have over the past couple of decades, it was possible to imagine that in a few years, a McMansion would be erected on every available inch of waterfront property, and instead of tackle shops and family-run diners, the downtown Stonington stores would be housing Williams Sonomas and Talbots shops to cater to the new upper-class urban residents and tourists who would provide the town with its new livelihood. It's a scenario that has already occurred repeatedly in similar Connecticut towns, where tourism has replaced fishing as their main income. Places like Westport, Guilford, and Mystic are no longer the fishing communities they once were. It's terribly ironic how people keep reaching further and further away from the cities to find cozy and charming communities, and then once they get there, realize they don't like living in a place where the stores and restaurants close at 5:00 p.m. on a Sunday, if they were open on a Sunday at all. So they bring in their bulldozers and chain stores and make a duplicate and smaller version of the community they wanted to escape from to begin with. The future was looming in front of me and I didn't like what I saw.

I took a deep breath, closed my eyes, and drank in the moment. When I opened my eyes, I looked up at the bright blue sky and suddenly the future was a long way away. At this point, the suburban mansions weren't there, and as far as I knew, the closest McDonald's was in Bangor. Now is what matters. What the future brings is irrelevant. Never have I been able to get the "big picture" out of my head more quickly than I did that day. Maybe there was magic present after all?

As we left the house, Brenda wanted me to be sure to right one wrong that had been done with *Travels with Charley*. In the book, Steinbeck mentioned picking up three lobsters for dinner one night, so I asked Brenda, "By the way, who ate the third lobster?"

"Well, my aunt was rather shy, and since Elizabeth Otis knew this, she didn't tell my aunt that Steinbeck was coming to visit until the day before he was due to arrive. Since he was already on his way, my aunt couldn't stop him from coming, so in a bit of a panic, she called her friend, Madeleine Burrage, to be here with her. I guess Madeleine was rather put out that she wasn't mentioned in the book, so I'd really appreciate it if you could mention her."

Done.

Brenda wanted to meet Judy, so we shut Gabi in the house, and walked up the slight grade to Roxie II.

"You know, you parked in the same place John Steinbeck did," she said with a little surprise.

"I did?!" I said with even more surprise.

"Yes. He parked right about where you're parked and he stayed in the truck for two nights."

I looked around the large property and thought of how many other places I could have chosen to park—literally anywhere, really. I'm not one to normally put much weight into coincidences or serendipitous moments, but I have to admit I felt a slight shiver go up my spine. Suddenly, Steinbeck's impression of the mysticism of Deer Isle started to make more sense to me.

Judy was eager and thrilled to meet Brenda and was even more overjoyed to have her belly rubbed several hundred times while Brenda and I finished up our visit. Just after noon, Judy and I found ourselves rattling back over the high bridge and away from Deer Isle. As we headed toward Bar Harbor and the *Queen Mary 2*, I, like Steinbeck, felt like a part of my soul had been touched, and longed to return.

Sadly, the calm and serenity of Deer Isle diminished rapidly once I got back on the mainland. En-route to the dock that housed the view of my first non-dry-docked ocean liner, I hit traffic. Big traffic. Rush hour-like traffic. It appeared the entire eastern seaboard was also interested in seeing the *Queen Mary 2*.

Since I had already lost two days with the breakdown back in Massachusetts, I really was worried about time. It seemed to be slipping away faster every single day, and I still had a long way to go in a short period of time. Could I really afford to wait another day to get to upper Maine? What if I ran into trouble there? Would I lose a day for every day I was on the road? Maybe spontaneous detours like this *Queen Mary 2* visit were not only unnecessary, but also detrimental to being able to actually finish the trip. I pulled out the map again and realized if I didn't take the two days to go to northern Maine, and instead turned west from where I was, I could be in Niagara Falls the following day and effectively back on my original schedule. After moving about a half mile in the better part of an hour, I decided to give up on the *Queen Mary 2* and on northern Maine. Sad and tired, I turned Roxie II around and left the Atlantic coast, finally starting my westward trek toward the Pacific Ocean and all sites between.

That night I drove hurriedly back across Maine and into New Hampshire. I had originally wanted to go back to the camp site in New Hampshire where we had spent Saturday night, but when I called for a reservation, the owners informed me that dogs were not allowed in cabins, and they weren't terribly happy with the fact that I neglected to mention that to them when I stayed there on Saturday. I decided instead to try to get as many miles behind us as we could. I had been traveling close to a week and was still in the Eastern Time Zone. It was starting to feel like I was never going to get out of New England. We finally stopped after dark in St. Albans, Vermont. The only motel with a vacancy did not allow dogs, so I decide to live on the edge. I didn't tell them about Judy. I was too tired to continue driving, and to be honest, I knew Judy wouldn't do any damage to the place, nor would she bark, so I figured what the heck. The worst thing they could do would be to kick me out and never let me back again. Eh. Join the club.

St. Albans, Vermont, to Erie, Pennsylvania
Tuesday, September 28, 2004

I woke up rested, and tremendously excited to get on the road. Today promised viewing of the legendary Niagara Falls! Millions of people have honeymooned there, and over a dozen people have gone over it in a barrel. Why, on either count? Who knows? But it's big and rushing and loud and wet and exciting and international and I couldn't wait.

It was odd to, suddenly, have the trip be secondary to the destination. Even Judy seemed unusually eager to get there. The mighty falls beckoned, and we were on the move.

We started our day at a local gas station that had not only a restaurant, but the most unhappy waitress I've ever met in my life. The service was slow, the food was horrible, and I believe the waitress literally growled at me. It amazes me how many people are so miserable in their daily lives and they either don't know it, or they've just given up. Just what could have made this woman so wretched that she not only wallowed in her misery, but to also infect as much of the entire universe as she could is something I'm glad I don't know. She reminded me of the waitress Steinbeck met just outside of Bangor. He wrote: "Then there are others, and this dame was one of them, who can drain off energy and joy, can suck pleasure dry and get no sustenance from it. Such people spread a grayness in the air about them."

Vermont was particularly lazy that autumn afternoon. The fall colors were just starting to peek out of their summer greenery, and we drove through sleepy town after sleepy town nary seeing a soul. In a couple of months, though, this lovely area would be mobbed with skiers and snowboarders when the winter snow season began. I was delightfully surprised when we drove past one of the few drive-in movie theaters left in the country. In 1960, they were in practically every town, but due to technological advancements, in 2004 folks seemed to prefer seeing their movies on their home theater systems or in controlled-climate cinemas with state-of-the-art THX sound systems rather than being crunched in a hot car, swatting at mosquitoes, and listening to *Pirates of the Caribbean: The Curse of the Black Pearl* through a staticky mono speaker hanging from the car window. I had some great times at drive-ins during my youth and teen years. The fact that there are millions of people today who will never know the joys of watching movies with their friends outside under the stars, and yet still be in the semi-privacy of their own car, well, it just made me sad. It also makes me wonder just where do teens go to make out these days? They must be going somewhere, and wherever it is, it's likely more private than the back seat of a 1962 Chevy Impala at a drive-in.

We finally crossed into New York State at Rouses Point, just shy of the Canadian border. The farms in upstate New York were starting to remind me of my youth in the Midwest. Growing up in Nebraska, I remembered the square bales of hay that used to speckle the ground every few feet where the baler had spit them out. Trucks would come by later and pick them up one at a time, then drive them back to the barn where they were stored up high in the haymow. My friends and I would spend hours playing in the barn—we'd start by climbing to the top of the highest bale in the highest part of the hayloft. Then we'd jump down, down, down until we were at the bottom of the haystack. From there, we would drop into the shoots to the feed bins, climb through the window into the lower barn, jump to the ground, then run outside, up the hill, and back into the big barn to climb the ladder and do it all over again. We could, and would, entertain ourselves like that for hours.

Here in New York, though, it appeared that children were denied the same energetic afternoon activities with hay bales. These large fields were full of huge round hay bales shrink-wrapped with white plastic to keep out moisture through the winter, and looking about as mobile as a silo. Instead of looking like pieces of Chex Mix scattered on the ground, these monoliths looked more like giant marshmallows in a field of broken Shredded Wheat. All it lacked was snow to make it Frosted Shredded Wheat.

We hit Buffalo, New York, just in time for rush hour and ended up in our first traffic jam since the *Queen Mary 2*. I was surprised to find that you can see Niagara Falls long before you hear it. I always thought it would be the other way around, but the mist from the falls rises so high up into the air, you can see it from miles and miles away.

As we sat there stalled in traffic, I tried to remember as much as I could about the falls, since all Steinbeck told us about them was that he was glad to have seen them, so if anyone ever asked him if he had been there, he could say, "Yes, and be telling the truth for once." I've always thought it strange that he didn't extrapolate on the largest Niagara Falls story of that year and quite possibly, ever.

On July 9, 1960, a seven-year-old boy named Roger Woodward was thrown from a small boat that capsized on the Niagara River just above the falls. He went over the falls and was plucked out of the water below by the *Maid of the Mist* tour boat. He was the first person to have ever gone over the falls unprotected and survived.

Think about it...the Horseshoe Falls are 170 feet high. That's the equivalent of a 17-story building! Add to that, six million cubit feet of water from Lake Erie going over the falls every minute and pounding onto massive rocks at the bottom as it makes its rushing way north toward Lake Ontario. Suddenly, a little boy, wearing only a life jacket and a swimsuit gets swept into the 25 mph currents and is washed over the rim to certain death. Hundreds of people witness the event, horrified. Moments later, the *Maid of the Mist* captain spotted a bright orange life jacket bobbing in the water below and rushed over to pick up the boy. It was expected that he was either already dead or at least fatally injured. Against all odds, Roger didn't have a single broken bone or major laceration and walked away with only a slight concussion. Maybe it's me, but I was completely boggled and awed at the story, and it was at the forefront of my mind as I slowly inched my way toward the scene of the miracle from nearly a half-century before.

And yet, three months after the phenomenal incident, Steinbeck laid eyes on the mighty and murderous falls in person for the first time, and wrote...nothing.

I have always been fascinated with the daredevil history of the falls. I remember being about five years old when my grandmother told me about people going over the falls in a barrel, and my response was, "Why?" I couldn't understand why anyone would want to go over a waterfall, since they were obviously put on earth for their aesthetic value only, and why a barrel? Wouldn't a boat make more sense? Now, granted I didn't fully understand the physics involved in tumbling waterfalls, but the logic of my five-year-old brain dictated that since boats floated on top of water, that they would stay on top of the water throughout the whole over-the-falls journey. A barrel would just roll over and over and make you dizzy. It certainly seemed like a stupid pursuit to me. And who would start such a silly thing? I blame Annie Edison Taylor.

In 1901, Annie Taylor was the first person to go over the falls in a barrel and survive. She climbed into an airtight wooden barrel with the air pressure pumped to 30 psi with a bicycle pump, and oopsy-daisy, over the falls she fell into hopeful fame and riches. Alas, she died in poverty, but over a century later, her insanity lives on with subsequent copycat daredevils. Some lived. Some didn't. Some went alone. Some went with friends. A couple of people even did it twice for some unknown reason. And yet, I'm fascinated by the stories. Were these merely adrenaline junkies searching for fame and riches, too? Or were they suicidal people who decided to leave it up to the gods and goddesses as to whether they lived or died? Regardless of the motivation, I think they were all fools. And yet, fascinating fools nonetheless.

I knew that the view was better from the Canadian side, so I decided to pop over to get a gander at the American, Bridal Veil, and Horseshoe Falls. Steinbeck was unable to enter Canada due to not having a vaccination certificate for Charley, and I was wondering if I would have similar issues. Since he gave me the tip-off on carrying paperwork for the dog, I had Judy's current shot records at the ready, and I joined the line of cars crossing the no-man's-land bridge into the Great White North. As I approached the Canadian border, I saw the familiar Maple Leaf flag flying proudly over the checkpoint, however, when Steinbeck was in this exact same spot, he didn't. In fact, there was a much different flag flying in 1960—the Union Jack. The Maple Leaf flag was not adopted as the national flag of Canada until 1965. To my 21st Century eyes, it would have been incredibly weird to see any other icon representing our neighbors to the north, and yet my parents did. It's sort of like the 48-star American flag that my grandparents owned. It was a major part of their lives, but not mine.

I zipped into Canada without any issues, and that delightfully surprised me, however I did need my passport to cross the border. In the pre-9/11 world, Steinbeck had no such restriction. Back then, only dogs weren't allowed to travel internationally without papers.

When I finally arrived at the falls themselves, I was shocked to see a giant Hershey bar blocking my view! It was the entrance to a massive candy store that was attached to other massive stores offering every sort of family entertainment to the millions of tourists who flock there annually. It reminded me of a less-neon-y Vegas, and I was not only surprised, but rather sad to see it. I was under the impression that the falls were a honeymoon destination, full of quaint bungalows with romantic views of the falls as backdrops for newlyweds to gaze into each other's eyes and whisper tender endearments over candlelit dinners. But then again, that was how they were depicted over a half century earlier by Hollywood. Once again, I needed to kick myself for believing what I saw in movies.

After driving around a bit, I finally found my way to a parking spot on Goat Island. After securing the perimeter of any unsavory—or even friendly—canine, I opened Roxie and let Judy out. I was wondering how she would handle getting close to that much rushing water and anticipated she wouldn't want to get too near. Together we walked to the railing that marked the edge of Horseshoe Falls. Judy sniffed the ground back and forth, wagged her tail and beamed up at all people who walked by. Occasionally someone would succumb to her flirtatious looks and stop to pet her. She immediately would drop to the ground, roll over on her back, and allow them to administer a much appreciated belly rub. I kept expecting Judy to put on the brakes and refuse to get any closer to the falls, but she seemed oblivious to the water spraying in her face and the roar of the falls getting louder and louder like a lion approaching from the distance. She might as well have been running around in her own backyard, as much attention as she was paying to one of nature's most amazing creations. I, however, got more and more nervous with each step. I've been known to be vulnerable to vertigo at times, and the closer I got to the edge of the falls, the more I felt that strange sensation of being drawn over the railing, into the rushing water, and plummeting to the bottom. I slowed. Then I stopped altogether. I was still a good ten yards from the railing, but it was close enough for me. Judy sneezed a bit and smiled up at me while wagging her rear end. I think she must have known I was nervous, bless her heart. I reached down to pet her and up came her belly. I chuckled and obeyed.

After the earlier excitement of the traffic jam followed up by the majestic natural sites, leaving Niagara Falls was rather anticlimactic. After a quiet dinner with friends in Buffalo, we continued south along Interstate 90. I finally stopped in Erie, PA, for the night. We were finally back on schedule. I slept well.

Erie, Pennsylvania, to Rockford, Illinois
Wednesday, September 29, 2004

An overcast sky greeted me in the morning. Now that I was back on schedule, the pressure of time was alleviated for the moment. I took my time getting going in the morning and leisurely wrote my blog entry over coffee and a donut. I thought what I had written was tremendously witty and entertaining and was eager to get it posted to my web page so people all around the world would be able to enjoy it as well. I asked at the motel desk if there was any place I could find Internet access. The friendly clerk eagerly told me about the city's new wireless "hot spot" on its town green. I had my doubts about this new form of technology, but decided to give it a try anyway.

As I drove toward the town green, I passed yet another Model A Ford! It was just chugging along the road, happy as can be, as if it was in its normal habitat. I was grinning at the serendipity of it all when I saw the frogs.

Since the early 1960s, towns and cities across America have embarked on a type of community pride art project. The town decides on a theme for outdoor sculptures that represent the community, create a whole bunch of basic models, and then hold a contest for artistic citizens to modify for eventual public display. These art competitions are usually held in conjunction with their local fair or some other festival. For example, St. Paul, Minnesota, is the birthplace of Charles Schultz, so they have lots of Snoopy, Charlie Brown, and Lucy sculptures scattered around in various places. In Erie, Pennsylvania, they had frogs.

There were frogs everywhere downtown. A "One-Frog Band" complete with trumpets coming out of his eyes, and a keyboard for teeth. A "Long-horned Bullfrog" with horns and a ring in its nose, was safely ensconced in its own bullpen. They all seemed a little creepy to me because the frogs weren't sitting down like frogs do. They were standing on their hind legs like a human. The statues were well over six feet high so they cast an imposing presence. After walking around the green and taking photos of as many frogs as I could, I settled into Roxie II to upload my blog.

To my joy and amazement, it worked! It was my very first wireless up-load to the Internet ever! It made me feel all giddy and terribly excited. I mean, if it was possible to send documents through the air like Willy Wonka sent Mike TV across the room, could Never-Ending Gobstoppers and lickable wallpaper be far behind?

Judy was itching to get out and sniff the frogs herself, so I put away my computer and grabbed her leash. While we were walking toward a monument dedicated to war veterans, a news vehicle pulled up across the street and two gentlemen got out. I thought that they might be interested in Judy's and my story, so I went over and introduced myself. Not only were they interested in our story, but one of the gentlemen was also a huge dog lover—in particular, two *bleu*-merle Pomeranians who lived with him. I'd never even heard of *bleu*-merle Pomeranians! How cute they must be! I told him about the dramas of our first days on the road, the de-mise of the original Roxie, and our excursion to Holy Smokes BBQ. Then he surprised me again and told me of another restaurant that he knew of in Pennsylvania that was also located in a deconsecrated church. Con-sidering the Model A Ford I saw earlier in the day, I started feeling that Erie is really located in a somewhat parallel universe, perhaps a wrinkle in time where everything is relatively the same, but slightly not. A place where information mysteriously transmits through air, your recent past repeats itself, and frogs walk on two legs. A magical place to be sure.

I left the Midwest's Brigadoon late. As a result, I really had to minimize my stops for the rest of the day, even though road-weariness was taking hold. I'd been on the road for almost a week and I was in desperate need of a day off. Steinbeck stopped to rest in Chicago, but since I had family in the Twin Cities, I decided to take my much-needed break there instead. Unfortunately, that meant one more extra day on the road first.

I left Pennsylvania, drove through Ohio, across Indiana, and ended my day at Rockford, Illinois. I drove entirely on the Interstate. As Steinbeck so famously predicted in 1960, that once the Interstate system was completed it would be possible to drive from New York to California and not see a single thing, I found it to be very true on this particular turnpike.

Of course, when one's mind is free from visual distractions of quaint villages, views of rustic farmlands, or scenic wetlands, it is free to roam the world of inner thoughts. Spending a lot of time driving on a stress-free, two-lane highway, I find I actually get a lot of things done. I have accepted an Academy Award, climbed Mount Everest, gone on a date with George Clooney, added an addition to my house complete with swimming pool, bowling alley, and gift-wrapping room, been interviewed by Oprah, built an orphanage in India, won an LPGA tournament, and been sworn in as President of the United States.

Rockford, Illinois, to Minneapolis, Minnesota
Thursday, September 30, 2004

I was up with the birds and on the road with the sunrise. My destination that day was the World Famous Wisconsin Dells. But first, I had a mission—candy.

John Steinbeck mentioned a strange brand of candy that he saw as he traveled through the beautiful state of Wisconsin. He said no one would believe him when he told them about it, and I was determined to find out if he was telling the truth or not. After all, he apparently used to lie about having seen Niagara Falls; therefore his word was a little sketchy. I made my first stop at the Mousehouse Cheesehaus in Windsor, Wisconsin. It certainly looked like a good place to start. Surely a place with a 10-foot 3D mouse statue looming over the entrance would have at least heard of the existence of Swiss Cheese Candy.

Yes, I was looking for something that I didn't even think existed. But boy, if it did, I sure wanted to know what it tasted like. Would it be shaped like a piece of Swiss cheese, or would it be more candy-shaped and just have the flavor of Swiss cheese? I wanted to know.

Lucky for me, the owners had indeed heard of the treat. They even remembered the name of the company that used to make it, Mayville Cheese Company. However, they told me the company had since gone out of business. At least that's their story. Maybe they've "seen" Niagara Falls, too.

Having got that important tidbit unsatisfactorily settled, I shifted my focus to the store and all the glorious trappings within. Not only were there at least 10,000 different cheeses available, but they also sold awesome kitschy souvenirs! Cheese hats, shot glasses, back scratchers, etc., surrounded me. I felt like I was in a Stuckey's truck stop in 1976. I spent the better part of an hour perusing the fabulous wares, and periodically squealing with delight like a schoolgirl. There really are very few things in life more entertaining than looking at the tackiest souvenirs specially made for hick travelers like me. You really can't put enough glitter on a back scratcher that is shaped like a hand and has a tassel hanging from the other end, with a picture of a piece of cheese in the middle. Nope. Not for this girl anyway.

Several dozen dollars lighter (after all, I hadn't gotten my relatives anything from my trip yet, and the snow globes would be perfect stocking stuffers at Christmas), I was rolling down Interstate 94 and following the "Wisconsin Dells" signs. Not long after I left the highway, I found myself driving along a thruway for miles that was lined with motels, hotels, indoor water parks, Ferris wheels—some things called "ducks" that looked like small ferry boats with wheels—ooh, look! There was a giant Pink Flamingo! A giant roller coaster shaped like a Trojan Horse! An upside-down White House?! Just what the heck was this place? It had the feel of a Vegas/Disneyland love child. From the quiet depiction of the area in *Travels with Charley*, I was not exactly expecting this sort of hyperactivity, nor this many people. Steinbeck had spoken of the area as deserted and peaceful. He even spent the night camping near a flock of wild turkeys. This Upper Midwestern carnival midway was anything but. I was puzzled until I found a local fellow who told me that until recently, the Dells were merely a summer resort and after Labor Day it used to become a ghost town. Motels were vacant, rides were closed, and stores were shuttered while their owners flew to warmer weather for the winter. However, with the recent addition of the large scale, indoor water theme parks, it has become a year-round destination.

I also found that the Dells of the Wisconsin River were formed when the ice dam of the prehistoric Glacial Lake Wisconsin burst and the catastrophic flood etched through the Cambrian sandstone approximately 15,000 years ago. The water eventually headed down the Mississippi River and to the Gulf of Mexico. What it left behind is some of the most amazing rock formations in the country. The five-mile gorge is a popular tourist area and in 1994 was designated a State Natural Area by the Wisconsin State of Natural Resources.

I finally pulled over for a breather along the river. We parked in the Mexicali Rose restaurant parking lot and Judy and I took a walk. The river truly was beautiful, and I could get a glimpse of the scenic rock outcroppings a bit upstream. An amphibious vehicle (one of the "ducks", or a DUKW for you military purists) slowly passed by on its way downstream. I had never been more upset about my time limitations so far on the trip. I wanted to take a boat ride and see the glories of nature—the remnants of the mighty glaciers that melted millions of years ago after cutting through the Midwest and shaving down the earth to create the Great Plains.

The sun shone brightly, and all too soon, it was time to get on the road. Judy and I hopped back in the van and headed back toward the highway. Dinner at Buca di Beppo in downtown Minneapolis with family and friends awaited me; and eggplant parmesan with a bottle of wine sounded like an acceptable substitute to missing out on our dream vacation in the Dells.

The Twin Cities, Minnesota
Friday and Saturday, October 1-2, 2004

I woke up late on Friday morning at my friend's place in the cathedral section of St. Paul feeling depressed. After a wonderful dinner the night before, I awoke to a dark, cold, and rainy day. I had laundry to do, and I needed to review my next leg of the journey. Mainly I was tired. I'd been driving 10-hour days for a week and I was exhausted. I switched on the television and sat there for the entire day. I don't remember what I watched and it really doesn't matter. I didn't care about much of anything that day, except I knew I didn't want to get back on the road the next morning. It was too soon. And so I settled in for more TV.

Saturday was a different day, however. It was still cold, rainy, and depressing, but I actually felt alert enough to venture outside a bit. I realized that even after living in the Twin Cities for 15 years, I'd never been to F. Scott Fitzgerald's birthplace. The apartment I was staying in was only about five blocks away from it, so Judy and I suited up in our rain gear and headed out.

It's funny how some books, once read, can never truly leave you. It had been a good twenty years since I'd read *The Great Gatsby*, but as I walked along Western Avenue I could recall every character name and plot point as if I'd read it yesterday. I decided to take the long route to 481 Laurel Avenue so I continued on down Western Avenue to Summit Avenue and walked past two other of Fitzgerald's homes, 593 and 599 Summit Avenue.

Summit Avenue is a wide street that is lined with beautiful mansions that were built around the end of the 19th century. For a few blocks, most of the large homes are now historical sites. The Governor's Mansion is just a few blocks past Fitzgerald's place.

How amazing it must have been to have seen this area in its heyday. How different life must have been here at the beginnings of the 20th century. Dirt roads. Horse-drawn carriages. Parasols and top hats. The elite were truly the elite, and the rest of us were not. These mansions were bigger then than they are now, even though they haven't changed size. Family fortunes ended up getting dispersed throughout the generations and with the rise of the middle class, the dividing line between elite and middle class became fuzzy. After the Great Depression, the wealthy abandoned the city for the quiet of the suburbs, and these mansions were divided up into apartments or condos. Affluent addresses in downtown Minneapolis and St. Paul fell into ruin and decay. Ironically, in 2004, it was possible for me to actually live in one of these mansions—in 1904 I wouldn't even have been a guest in one. It's a beautiful street. It was getting cold, so I started hurrying along. In a few minutes I turned the corner onto Laurel Avenue and walked the last few blocks to find the residence where F. Scott Fitzgerald took his first breath. It was a nice looking, three-story, multi-family building. It had been well maintained over the years, and I'm sure the apartments there now were still expensive. A small plaque was attached to the wall next to the front steps that declared the home to be an historical location. That was it. I don't know what I was expecting to find. I did have the urge to knock on the door and ask for Old Sport, but it washed away with the rain. "I know myself, but that is all."

Then again, the dreariness of the day certainly wasn't helping, neither was the fact that everyone I hoped to see during my short time in town were all working or busy with their families or other responsibilities and so I was alone all day. I guess I was hoping for a flag flying, marching band, ticker-tape parade kind of homecoming, but instead I found that I was no longer a major part of these people's day-to-day lives. In the seven years since I'd moved away, my friends and family had moved on. I now knew how Steinbeck felt when he returned to his hometown of Salinas, California. He expected to find everything the same as when he left, but the people there had continued their lives, and the world they currently inhabited didn't include him. He felt like a ghost. Steinbeck was right to quote Thomas Wolfe. You really can't go home again. Lordy, it was depressing.

As I stood there on the sidewalk on Laurel Avenue wallowing in self-pity, I felt a soft nudge on my knee. I looked down and gazing up at me with loving eyes was a very wet and soggy Judy. She was right. It was time to go back to the apartment and pack. It was time to get back on the road.

St. Paul, Minnesota, to Detroit Lakes, Minnesota
Sunday, October 3, 2004

Who can turn the world on with her smile? No, it wasn't Mary Tyler Moore. It was my friend, Tami, handing me one of her company's very yummy cheesecakes for the next leg of my journey. Considering the name of her company is "Muddy Paws Cheesecake" it was a very fitting send-off. Judy enjoyed it, too.

I had one last task to do before I left the Twin Cities. Steinbeck mentioned that he wanted to find Golden Valley, Minnesota, because he liked the name. However, he got lost in the sea of trucks on the highway, so he never did find it. Being a former Minneapolitan, I knew exactly where Golden Valley was, and I wanted to be sure to succeed where Steinbeck so stupendously failed—and I wanted to photograph it for good measure. You know, in case someone would ever accuse me of having "seen" it in a Steinbeck-Niagara-Falls kind of way.

I got back on highway 94, swung through Minneapolis, picked up my sister and her camera, and we headed west on highway 7 through St. Louis Park. Finally, we found the sign designating the city of Golden Valley.

It's a suburb. It's mainly residential. It's pretty flat so I'm not really sure why it's called Golden Valley. We took some shots of the water tower and the strip mall that bore the town name, grabbed some breakfast, and got back on the road toward Detroit Lakes. It felt good to be on the road again, and for the first time, I truly felt like I was heading out on an adventure instead of just heading back home. It was also nice to have my sister as a companion for a few days. A little known fact about

Steinbeck's trip is he didn't travel it all alone as the book reads. His wife actually accompanied him on a large part of the journey, therefore I felt I wasn't doing him any disservice by inviting my sibling along for a bit. Judy is a swell passenger and all, but she's a crappy conversationalist.

We followed Steinbeck's path northwest toward Sauk Centre, Minnesota, which was the birthplace of Sinclair Lewis and the town upon which he based his book, *Main Street*. Sinclair Lewis was the first American to be awarded the Nobel Prize for Literature, and Steinbeck knew him well enough to meet him for lunch occasionally at the Algonquin Hotel in New York City, but still always called him "Mr. Lewis."

I have to admit I'm not even remotely a Sinclair Lewis fan. I know he wrote *Main Street* and *Babbit* and somehow in my head I also have him authoring *Death of a Salesman,* but I'm pretty sure I'm wrong on that last one. Anyway, I was never forced to read his stuff in school. At one point I did try to read *Main Street* because I thought it sounded interesting, but I got sort of bored with it while the doctor's wife was trying to create some sort of high society with the locals, and eventually one night I put it down to go to sleep, and never picked it up again. It's supposed to be a literary masterpiece, though, and I hear it caused quite a few ruffled feathers in Sauk Centre upon its publication. I was curious to see if this town revered or scorned its most famous former resident.

"THE SINCLAIR LEWIS INTERPRETIVE CENTER, NEXT RIGHT" read the billboard at the exit to town. So, I guess they were pretty proud of the old bugger now. I followed the signs to the center that was located in a charming little park, but unfortunately, the center was closed on Sundays. Judy and I took a brief walk around the park and even sniffed around the Judy-sized model of his birthplace located near the entrance before jumping back in Roxie II and driving down the most famous street in America—the original Main Street.

It looked like every other small town's main drag complete with a movie theater, restaurants, stores, and a gas station on the corner. I was looking for signs to direct me to his birthplace, but there were none. Finally I asked a lady who was waiting to cross the (Main) street where it was. She directed me to a lovely Victorian home that was set back from the road a bit. It was charming, but not simple. It appeared to be the home of a rather well-to-do family, but certainly not of anyone ostentatious. It certainly looked like what I imagined the doctor's home in *Main Street* would have looked like. There was a plaque on the door along with visiting hours, and according to this sign, it was open for business. I tried the screen door, but it was locked. I rang the doorbell. No answer. I knocked on the door and listened for footsteps, but to no avail. Finally, I walked along the lovely front porch and peeked in the windows. It looked very nice and I really wanted to get a tour, but I didn't see or hear a soul. It was frustrating. I was starting to feel like Clark Griswold in the movie, *Vacation*, only Sauk Centre was my "Wally World."

Slightly dejected and back on the road, I headed toward Detroit Lakes. I'd never been to Detroit Lakes. I've always known it to be a fishing town and I don't fish. Nor do I know anyone who fishes. Well, my grandfather used to fish and I really liked going fishing with him when I was about ten or so. It was great! My grandparents would load up their camper and haul it down to a river or lake and we'd pick up some worms from the local bait shop and go visit them for the day. Grandpa showed me how to bait the hook (he also showed me how to roll cigarettes when I was seven) and then I'd walk down to the edge of the water and cast the sinker-bobby thing out there as far as I could. That was truly the fun part of fishing, casting. You grab the fishing pole, hold the release lever down as far as you can, swing your arm back and simultaneously let the release lever go. The hook and bobber would sail in a smooth arc out over the water, the fishing line glistening in the early morning sun, before falling gently down to earth and landing with a quiet "plunk" in the dark, cool lake. And then we'd sit and wait. We didn't talk much because that's also a good part about fishing. It's about being in the moment, hearing the birds call across the mist as it rose off of the lake, smelling the freshness of the morning dew, and watching the water gently lap up on the shore— knowing you have nowhere else to be and are in no hurry to get there. Occasionally a fish would bite a hook, and that's when it gets exciting. Then it's about reeling the sucker in while it fights to get free of the hook, and I'm afraid I was never very good at that part. And so, once the fish would inevitably get loose and swim free, I'd reel in the line, Grandpa would put another worm on the hook, and I'd cast it out again, trying to get it ever further out than the last time. I miss fishing. I haven't done any at all since my grandfather passed away in 1977. I do have his old tackle box and rods, so I could go fishing anytime if I wanted to. I think the reason I liked it so much was because it was something I did with Grandpa. None of his other grandchildren seemed to like it as much as me, so it really was our special thing. I think I just miss Grandpa.

Detroit Lakes, Minnesota, to Dickinson, North Dakota
Monday, October 4, 2004

Detroit Lakes was the first time on the trip that it was truly cold. We awoke to frost, sunshine, and 30 degrees and it felt colder than that. I made a stop at a Kmart and purchased some new gloves before heading out towards Fargo. As I fueled up at a Conoco Station, I met a man named Jerry who told me about the name of the town. He said the strip of land between the two lakes is officially called a "Detroit." However, once they added water to the hole on either side of it and created lakes, they had to change the name of the town. I think he was full of it, but then again, he's probably a fisherman.

They say North Dakota has two seasons—winter and road construction. When I arrived in Fargo, I found that they were still in the latter season. I drove through town as quickly as I could because I was eager to get to Alice.

In 1950, the town of Alice had 162 residents. In 1960, Steinbeck said it had 124. As of the 2000 census, there were only 56. It was dying. Unfortunately, this was not an uncommon fate for small farming towns at the beginning of the 21st Century. The family farms that were once the literal bread and butter of this country have slowly been run out of business by the large-scale factory farms. It's a sad reality.

We pulled into town and very quickly found the Maple River, which is where Steinbeck said he camped for the night. Since there wasn't any clearly marked or logical spot for a campsite, I decided to find a local store and ask if anyone there had heard of any stories of where he might have stayed.

The first store I could find was located in nearby Chaffee, ND, next to the grain silos near the railroad tracks. I pulled up to the only store, restaurant, and bar in town, the Chaffee Café and Bronco Bar. Lucky for me, Don and Rick Schroeders were inside and they were not only eager to help me find the location I was searching for, but they also told me everything about the area that I could ever hope for.

To start off, Chaffee and Alice were located near an old wagon train trail. In fact, they told me you could still see the wagon ruts from a century and a half ago in the area where the main crossing point of the Maple River was. There was even an historical marker at the spot. It sounded like as good of a camping place as any, so they gave me directions to the crossing. Before I left, though, they strongly encouraged me to go see one of the area's must-see tourist attractions, The Can Pile.

The Can Pile is a 25-foot-high pile of oilcans that was built in 1933 by a man named Max G. Taubert. It was originally located on highway 10, but when Interstate 94 was built, the community didn't want to see it destroyed, so they moved it to its current location, just off the highway in Casselton, ND. In 1960, Steinbeck would have driven right past it. It was very likely that he might have stopped at the gas station and got fuel or coffee. And yet, he mentioned none of it in *Travels with Charley*. Could that be because it wasn't as fabulous looking as the photo Don and Rick showed me in a book about the area? (It looked pretty amazing.) Or did Steinbeck not mention it because he just had no interest in that sort of kitschy Americana? I was intrigued. In fact, so much so, that I decided to turn around and go see this bizarre monument that Steinbeck failed to mention. But first, we needed to find the historic landmark on the Maple River.

After thanking Don and Rick for their invaluable information, we left the Chaffee Café and headed south. We followed the dirt roads as we were directed, and I was completely charmed by the area. After a couple of turns we lost sight of Chaffee, and there was nothing but fields in every direction. The sky loomed large and bright blue above me. I heard nothing but the wind and the rustling of grasses and crops. There weren't even any farmers working on large combines anywhere. It was exhilarating! It had been a while since I'd felt that small and insignificant and awed by the majesty of nature, but it was also a comfort realizing that the world truly doesn't revolve around me. I had no control over anything at this point. If the van broke down, I would be stranded there on the side of that dirt road, quite possibly for days, until someone else came along and found me. Of course, once someone did come around, I know they would have lent a hand and helped me get going again, but that didn't make me feel any more secure in my solitude. Some people think they need to climb mountains in the Himalaya in order to feel that sort of humility, but all they really need to do is get lost on the prairie once.

I finally pulled into the little park area where the historical crossing was. It was very cute with a picnic table, shady trees along the river, and, as promised, an historic plaque describing the relevance of the location. It felt much warmer and inhabited than the road on the way there, and there was even a friendly farmer on a tractor passing by, who nodded hello. It was time to eat, so I made myself some lunch, and while I was eating, I did something I'd never done before—I let Judy off the leash in an unfenced area.

I was nervous as I reached down to unclip the leash, but Judy wasn't. She was so giddy, she ran around in circles at first and sniffed everything in sight. I can't imagine what she smelled, but she flopped on her back and did a version of doggie break dancing in the middle of what I can only assume smelled like Chanel No 5, or perhaps Eau de Liverwurst. Then she flipped back upright with her ear perked back and a huge smile on her face, feeling, no doubt, rather pretty. Then she was back up running and sniffing. This continued on for about an hour while I took in the beautiful autumn afternoon. The sun was beaming down with beauteous warm light and the grass smelled sweet and fresh. Soon, though, frost would set in and winter would be on its way.

I loaded up the van and we headed back on highway 94 toward Casselton. Rick and Don were specific in their directions, so I had no trouble finding the tower, excuse me...pile of cans. No. It really was a tower. It was silver and had the shape of a 15-tier wedding cake and was several stories high. What looked like chicken wire held the whole thing together and it was topped with a small flag. As I got closer, I noticed there was a list to it—the whole thing leaned like the Tower of Pisa, which I initially thought was due to it being moved, but as I later found out, was the result of a tornado. I was enthralled. The sunlight shimmered off the metallic paint of the cans and illuminated the surroundings with joy and good will. Just gazing upon this iridescent beacon of hope filled me with love and peace that would last me clear through until Wednesday.

As with all religious moments, it was ephemeral, and the gorgeous vision ultimately faded with the sun. Perhaps it was all just a dream?

I turned Roxie II around once again and headed back west. Steinbeck had mentioned that crossing the Missouri River in Bismarck was the true delineation of East and West. Up to this point, everything felt civilized and populated, but just crossing this river thrust one fully into the Wild West. Gosh darn, if that old Steinbeck son-of-a-gun wasn't right. Shucks, I'd no sooner forded that stream than I was hungrier than a pack of wolves at a sheep convention, so I ambled into a local cookhouse and ordered up some grub.

"Oh hi there! What can I getcha?" the pretty blond waitress said.

"Can I get the hot beef sandwich with the gravy on the side?" I asked.

"Oh, sure. You betcha!"

Well, that settled one thing I was hoping to find out on this trip. Steinbeck predicted that with the new highway system and the permeation of television and radio, that local dialects would ultimately disappear. Due to nationally syndicated radio, throughout the whole journey, I listened to the same radio stations: The River, The Wolf, The Edge, KROQ, Star, KIIS-FM etc. The DJs all sounded like they went to the same high school. And yet, even with the consolidation of radio, television, movies, travel, the Internet, and all sorts of inter-regional dialects bombarding people on a daily basis, here in North Dakota, people still retained the strong lilt of the area's Scandinavian roots. There certainly wasn't a dearth of dialect in North Dakota. It was like music to my ears, with gravy on the side.

Full of wonderful, heavy, fat-laden, luscious, artery-clogging goodness, I continued the drive toward Montana. The landscape was rather unchanging, with field after field of various crops hugging the narrow band of road. Corn, soybeans, wheat, milo, beans of all types, and probably everything else you find on your grocer's shelves grew in every direction for miles and miles, and after a while, road fatigue started to set in so I decided to stop for the night in Dickinson, ND.

I stopped at the first motel I saw with a vacancy sign. This motel was a huge turning point in my trip—the fact that I had a dog with me was not only not an issue, but the owner waived Judy's fee. She said it was because she didn't know how to work the new cash register system that had recently been installed to add the additional dog fee, but I think it was because Judy was so cute. Whatever the reason, Dickinson, North Dakota, was the starting point of dog-friendly accommodations for the rest of the trip. From this point on, until I returned to New England, I never had to pay extra for Judy at a motel. It was also my first glimpse at gracious western hospitality, which I have to say never failed to impress and delight me.

Dickinson, North Dakota, to Livingston, Montana
Tuesday, October 5, 2004

The morning started with a fabulous breakfast at a local restaurant. I decided to get pancakes with sugar-free syrup. I wanted to be sure to have a good solid base to last me a while because I was excited to get to the Badlands and I didn't want to make extra stops if possible. I left Dickinson at a good hour, eagerly touring down the road, when after about 30 or 40 miles my stomach started acting up. It wasn't anything resembling nausea or food poisoning. It was more like a dull pain from some strange intestinal malady, and it was excruciatingly uncomfortable. As minutes went by, the pain intensified. I felt pressure building up in my abdomen that kept getting stronger and stronger, and eventually I was sure my stomach would just pop and what was left of me would go zipping through the air like a balloon. Sure enough, that's what eventually happened, except it was more of a long, slow leak over the next few hours. I know pancakes don't normally affect me that way, but apparently sugar-free syrup has some sort of evil ingredient that mingles with your stomach acid and fizzes up like a shaken bottle of Coke. That day I drove with the windows wide open and Judy stayed in the back of the van.

The Theodore Roosevelt National Park is located in western North Dakota. It was established as a national park in 1978, although it had been known as The Theodore Roosevelt National Memorial Park since 1947. It is smack dab in the middle of the Badlands. I have no doubt Steinbeck spent his last night in North Dakota camping in this beautiful place. He described the Badlands as harsh and unyielding, stark and barren during the day, but when the sun set, the Badlands came alive with light and color and became more hospitable and welcoming after dark. He found it to be hypnotizing.

Having reached the park not long after my gaseous breakfast, I wasn't allowed the opportunity to see the Badlands in their magical state of dusk and sparkly-starriness, but I found them extremely pleasant enough during the day. From the visitor center's outlook, the landscape was truly romantic. The crags and gullies carved the rock into brilliant colors of oranges, reds, and browns, and the early morning sun cast long shadows to the west. The contrast gave the illusion of some of the gullies being bottomless, while others seemed to glow from within. The colors were spectacular. I lingered longer than I anticipated, partially because I knew I was at the end of North Dakota and I was hesitant to leave. I had met some of the most warm and wonderful people in my two days in the state and I knew there was much more to be discovered if only I could take the time. (Also, I was hesitant to leave the very clean restroom facilities behind because who knew what sort of public potty horrors were ahead of me.) But, alas, time was not my friend on this journey, so after a quick stop at a rest area to give Judy time to say adios in her own special way, we got back on highway 94 and gracefully eased into Big Sky Country.

I LOVE MONTANA.

I was completely blown away from the get-go. From beginning to end, Montana is one of the most beautiful places in the world. It truly has it all, big skies, misty mountaintops, vast prairies, raging rivers, cool lakes, snow-covered glaciers, and no speed limit.

I was very excited to get to Billings because Steinbeck said he bought a hat there. I really wanted to treat myself to an awesome leather cowboy hat—maybe with a studded, rhinestoned, or beaded band, so I was wide awake as I cruised into the pleasant downtown. There were lots of turn-of-the-century brick buildings around, and they all looked very nice. They housed small, upscale boutiques, nice restaurants, and the like. Very pleasant, but where was my western wear store? I guess I suspected there'd be at least one downtown, and maybe even more than one. I circumnavigated the main street, each time expanding my orbit by a block. Suddenly, there, shining like a beacon of holiness was Rand's Custom Hats.

I practically screeched into the parking lot and ran up to the door. When I opened the door, I heard a jingle go off somewhere in the back of the store. It was cool and dark inside, and the place smelled of leather and oil. It was also quiet. I felt like I was walking into a church. Then I saw the hats. Every color, shape, and size you could imagine lined the walls from floor to ceiling: high brims, low brims, studded, embroidered, feathered, beaded. It was dazzling. I was intoxicated.

I immediately felt my blood pressure drop as I slowly meandered through the store, caressing the calfskin, ostrich, alligator, and suede leathers, gently petting the feathers, and fingering the beading. Oh, how wonderful would it be to own one of these! And then I saw it—the hat that was made for me. It was a dark brown, low-brimmed hat with horsehair trim and chinstrap. It called to me like a siren song, and drew me close. I put it on. The heavens opened up and wrapped me in blessed holy light. I heard angels singing above whilst butterflies fluttered around my head. Somewhere in the world, daffodils bloomed, bunnies hopped, and a small child smiled the smile of purity, bliss, and hope. I had come home.

With one hand, I slowly took it off my head and turned it over to see the price, while I reached for my credit card with the other. Jesus, Mary and Joseph, could it really be $975?! A cloud drew over the sun and it started to rain; the butterflies died and fell to the earth; the daffodils withered and turned brown; and a small child pooped in his diaper. It was so beautiful, yet so out of reach. It was so unfair. I almost cried as I returned the hat to its resting place on the wall. Surely someone—someone would fall in love with it as much as I had and would give it a good home. Surely someone would.

I couldn't remain in this sad place, so I briskly turned on my heel and exited the store. I wasn't going to let myself cry. I just needed to pet a fluffy dog for a minute to remind me of what's important in life. I jumped into Roxie, grabbed Judy, and held her tight. She sensed my sorrow and tried to cheer me up with tail wags and slobbery kisses. I pulled my tear-streaked face out of her fur and looked her in the eye. She pulled her head back to gaze into my face to reassure me that she would always be there for me when she drew her lips back in a Judy smile, gave me another quick kiss on my nose, and then released a very large burp. That's all it took to make me laugh. I may have left Rand's Custom Hats bareheaded, but I also left it a little bit wiser. Happiness isn't a gorgeous, handmade, one-of-a-kind cowboy hat. Happiness is a warm puppy. (Although a hat like that would probably have made me happy for a while anyway. It sure was purdy.)

When I was a kid, I thought Yogi Bear lived in Yellowstone Park. (He lived in JELLYstone Park, for those of you who were just as confused as me.) It turns out that bears in Yellowstone were an issue for John Steinbeck as well. On his trip, Charley ditched his normal, mild-mannered, snooty French poodle upbringing and became a psycho wannabe bear-killer, which completely freaked Steinbeck out, since he'd never seen the evil side of his travel companion before. Steinbeck ended up aborting his trip to the national park and beelined back to Livingston for the night.

I already knew about the devil in my dog, and I also knew there was no way on God's green earth I was going to even try to camp in Yellowstone overnight. I had a limited amount of time to experience the park, so I knew I wasn't going to get much out of it on this trip. I was hoping maybe I might run into Boo Boo in the few minutes I was in the park, or at the very least, I would run into Ranger Smith at the gate. Sadly, neither happened.

The sun was setting rather quickly as I drove toward the park through the town of Red Lodge. Despite my race with the sun, I was completely blindsided by the level of charm present and I found my foot easing off the gas pedal. Adorable boutiques, quaint offices, and chic bistros lined the main street. Everything was clean and sparkling, and I could completely imagine myself living there. It was a small town, but it had a bit of a metropolitan feel. It was utterly charming. Did I mention it was charming?

Too soon we left the pristine loveliness of Red Lodge, and Roxie II rolled up the swervy road towards the heart of the park. The shadows got longer and longer, and I got a little seasick from that long and winding road. I don't know how far I drove, but it quickly became very obvious that I wouldn't be able to drive out again once it got dark. At least not without taking some serious risks regarding possibly hitting some wildlife, or just missing one of the many hairpin turns and rolling end over end down the mountain like the blue Mini Cooper did at the end of the original *The Italian Job*. No. It was better to just cut my losses for the day and find myself a nice motel back in Livingston and get a good night's sleep. Yes, that did sound much better than sleeping in the van and being rudely awakened by a bear or moose or Bigfoot scratching outside the door before smashing the window and crumpling the van like it was a tin can and devouring all the tasty morsels inside (i.e. me and Judy) as a midnight snack and then tossing the whole kit and kaboodle down the mountain, rolling end over end like the white Mini Cooper did at the end of the original *The Italian Job*. No, turning back sounded like a fine, fine idea.

In spite of my best efforts, on the way to Livingston, I was viciously attacked by every bug in Yellowstone Park, the state of Montana, and the three closest Canadian Provinces. Before I veered off the main road due to Roxie's windshield being opaque from the millions of dead bugs glued to its surface, and finding myself rolling end over end and bursting into flames, like the red Mini Cooper did at the end of the original *The Italian Job*, I found a gas station so I pulled over to scrape the dead bugs off the windows. The worst part is the families of all those bugs surrounded the van in mourning, and I was swarmed while trying to squeegee the little corpses off the windows so I could actually continue driving. Slapping myself silly and scratching my festering welts, I stumbled blindly back into the cab and gunned the motor.

As soon as I got back to a major highway, I saw the Livingston Inn Motel. It was a long, single-storied, Old West looking motel that ran alongside some railroad tracks, and a "Vacancy" sign hung outside.

I stepped into the friendly office and was greeted by a warm couple who identified themselves as the owners. Yes, there was a vacancy at a very affordable rate. Yes, dogs were welcome. In fact, they also had stables available if I had a horse. Yes, they had wireless Internet. Was I hungry? The room had a kitchen, and there was a restaurant and bar next door. Did I need any laundry done? There was a laundry available also. Was there anything else we would like?

"Could you please send George Clooney to my room to rub my feet?" I asked hopefully.

No, sadly they didn't have George. (Drat.) However, they had everything else. I couldn't believe how fabulous this place was. If only all motels had this kind of customer service.

Livingston, Montana, to Coeur d'Alene, Idaho
Wednesday, October 6, 2004

In the morning, after I paid my bill, I profusely thanked my splendid hosts, and departed with a piece of complimentary chocolate (I still can't believe they couldn't deliver George). Judy and I jumped in the cab and pointed Roxie II westward. Today it was all Interstate driving. For what I missed in scenery, I certainly made up in miles. Montana is a huge state, no matter how you drive it, and I was getting a little itchy to see the Pacific Ocean.

In a short while, I bumbled into Bozeman, which I've always considered the place where everyone who works at Yellowstone lives, you know, mountain climbers, mountain skiers...Mountain-Dew-types. Then again, historically it's also one of those Wild West cities. After my unfulfilling cowboy hat hunt in Billings, I was hopeful that I might find one in Bozeman. After all, I was now further west. Perhaps eastern gentrification and high-priced merchandise hadn't spread this far yet.

I took the first exit to Bozeman. At the end of the ramp, I saw a Target store. Behind it was a mall. Wha?? I felt like I was in suburban Connecticut again. Surely, there must be more to Bozeman than the same old boring neighborhoods I knew so well from Connecticut. Even after driving around for a while, I didn't find anything that would suggest we were anywhere specific—just another average-sized suburban city. Sure, it was nice and clean and homogenized, which isn't necessarily a bad thing, but I was hoping for more character. It was depressing. I hopped back on the highway with dwindling expectations to ever find any remnants of what once was the Wild West.

Later, on the way over the Rockies just before Butte, I saw a vision. I'm not a big believer in spiritual apparitions, but shimmering larger than life in the brilliant sunshine there shone a radiant, virginal white goddess. Not being Catholic, Lutheran, Episcopalian, or of any religious persuasion that has saints, martyrs, or symbolic "guardians," I found it rather odd that the heavens above would select me as the witness to this truly amazing miracle. She stood on the Continental Divide overlooking Butte with a delicate beauty, her arms at her sides with her palms lifted skyward as if to reach up for a warm, comforting embrace, such as a mother cradling a child. As I got closer, I realized it wasn't a vision at all, but a tangible, 90-foot, stone statue of...the Virgin Mary, perhaps? I was suddenly confused. I never thought of Montana as a bastion of Catholics, but perhaps I was mistaken. I was wrong once before, so it could possibly happen again.

Zipping down the mountain (wheee!) I screeched to a halt at the huge quarry that dominated the town and surrounding countryside. Mining! I hadn't thought of mining, actually. When I think of Butte, I think of a dangerous shoot-em-up, gun-swingin', saloon-brawlin', Wild West town. However, nothing in my viewpoint screamed "COWBOYS-R-HERE" like I expected it to. No one wore cowboy hats. I didn't see a single horse. I was disappointed yet again. There was a college—Montana Tech at the University of Montana. The college is very obviously a school that specialized in engineering. From the looks of it, I'd say mining engineering. I don't know what that particular science is called, but now that I was thinking about it, I realized it must be rather complicated.

First, you'd have to know about geology so you would understand where to mine. Then, you'd have to know about mechanical engineering and bearing loads and architecture and construction and all that. Then, you'd have to know about physics and how things like removing earth from here will affect the earth over there, and how much oxygen do workers need to be productive. Then, there must be some sort of classes on the psychology of the people who work in the mines like how much cubic feet of space does a person need for optimum work efficiency and minimum "flipping out and pick-axing their coworkers over a cigarette." Funny that I never thought about mining that much before, and now that it was right in front of me, I was fascinated. However, I still had western fantasizes I needed fulfilled, so I cruised around town searching for a glimpse of my first hot hunk o' horse wrangler.

Sadly, and surprisingly, I didn't see any. But how could that be? Butte was even proudly the home of The Dumas Brothel, country's longest-running house of prostitution (1880-1982). You'd think there'd be a stray cowboy or two still hanging around. Maybe there might be some in Missoula??

I was starting to get tired of Montana. Like any love affair, the infatuation was wearing off and I needed some space. I soldiered on. I didn't bother stopping in Missoula because I felt it would have been just another disappointment. From the viewpoint of the highway, it looked more industrial than either Butte or Billings. That didn't bode well for finding any cowboys, and so I passed it by. Time was once again on my tail, and I was ready for some serious Rocky Mountain highs.

Towards the end of Montana, the landscape started shifting. Instead of ranch land and scenic ore-filled buttes and mesas (what's the difference between a butte and a mesa anyway?) there were more hills covered with tall, skinny pine trees. Roxie II wound up the twisty roads, higher and higher into the mountains. The mist settled in over the evergreens. I was leaving the prairies and flatlands and climbing the one last hurdle to the Pacific Ocean. Logging trucks started appearing again, having been absent from the roads since New England. The air was cooler and moister. Autumn was settling in. Before I knew it, I was finally leaving the mighty and beautiful state of Montana and entering Idaho.

I didn't know what to expect of Idaho because at this point in *Travels with Charley* Charley took ill, so Steinbeck drove "hell for leather" to a veterinarian in Spokane. It's a shame because he missed out on spending some time in heaven on earth, otherwise known as Lake Coeur d'Alene.

I was gobsmacked as I rounded the bend above town. The sun was setting over the mountain and sparkled like a diamond on the cool mountain lake. Golden clouds twinkled in the twilight sky and sucked my breath right out of my body. The yellows, golds, and oranges of the sunset deepened and mist inched out over the calm water. Stars peeked out from under the purple blanket of sky. I slowed my drive to a crawl so I could watch God's handiwork as he gently eased the earth to slumber. If there truly is a heaven, I reasoned, it must surely look like this.

For the first time on this trip I stayed in a chain motel rather than an independent one. Mainly this choice was because I was still dazzled by the night and it was the first place I saw. I hurriedly checked in and then went to a local bar and grill for dinner. The restaurant was warm and welcoming. The food was hot and plentiful. The beer was cold and locally brewed. I felt myself slow down and relax for the first time in days. I felt like I was finally getting in the groove of road travel. I had a bit of a rhythm going. Get up in the morning, walk Judy, and get breakfast. Read the part of *Travels with Charley* that pertained to my day's trip. Hit the road and drive until I got tired. Grab dinner, write my blog, and go to sleep. The days were starting to blend together more, and my home life seemed like a dream I once had. It was nice to be in charge of my destiny, the captain of my ship, the lady of the manor...I didn't have any responsibilities except to myself, and once I got over the adjustment period, I found myself enjoying my newfound freedom. Then again, the atmosphere of the town made it easy to unwind. So did the two beers and large hamburger I had. Maybe if I just...stayed? I could call a realtor to sell my house and its belongings, and I'd just stay here indefinitely. Maybe I could take up fishing again; after all, if you teach a girl to fish, she'll eat for a lifetime! It sure sounded good to me. I even checked out what bands were coming to the bar in the next few weeks as if I might just hang around for a while. As I walked slowly back to the motel, I realized I was only dreaming. I had a job and responsibilities back home waiting for me, and if I ever wanted to move here, it would take more than just an "I'm not going back" decision. Jobs would need to be found, houses sold, and stuff shipped. To continue dreaming about the footloose and carefree life I was currently living as a permanent situation was impossible. But, it's hard to think about earthly responsibilities when you're hanging out in heaven, so I allowed myself one more night of delusion.

"The journey begins!" On the Long Island Sound ferry to Connecticut.
(Note the Model A Fords surrounding Roxie I.)

Just hours later, Roxie and I broke down in Hatfield, Massachusetts.

Vicki Cain

Deer Isle, Maine.

Vicki Cain

Deer Isle, Maine.

Vicki Cain

Brenda Gilchrist and myself at her Deer Isle home where John Steinbeck
visited Brenda's aunt, Miss Eleanor Brace.

Kathleen Cain Nastrom

Judy takes the wheel.

Frog in Erie, Pennsylvania.

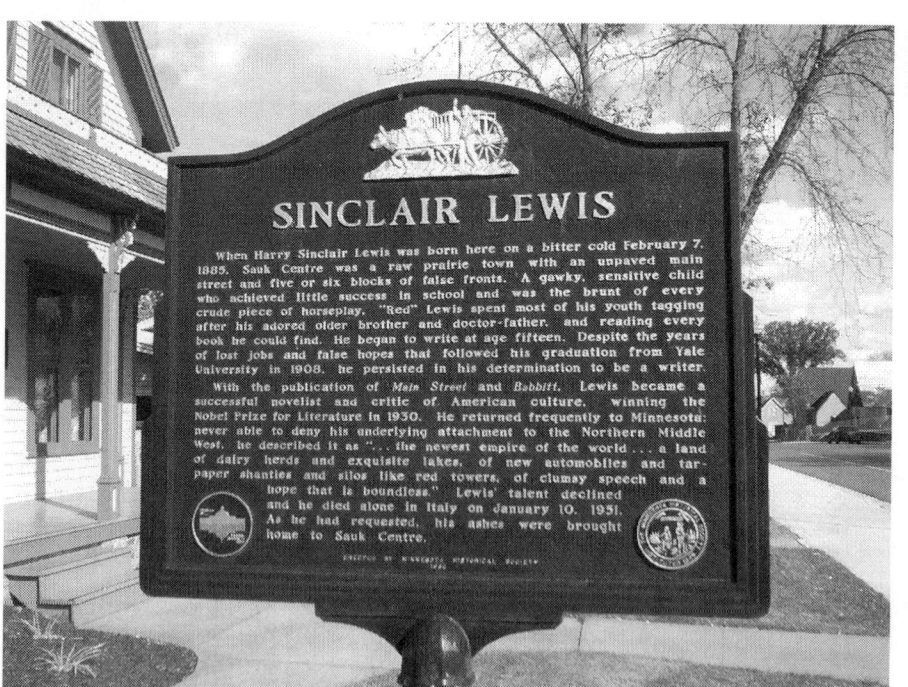

SINCLAIR LEWIS

When Harry Sinclair Lewis was born here on a bitter cold February 7, 1885, Sauk Centre was a raw prairie town with an unpaved main street and five or six blocks of false fronts. A gawky, sensitive child who achieved little success in school and was the brunt of every crude piece of horseplay, "Red" Lewis spent most of his youth tagging after his adored older brother and doctor-father, and reading every book he could find. He began to write at age fifteen. Despite the years of lost jobs and false hopes that followed his graduation from Yale University in 1908, he persisted in his determination to be a writer.

With the publication of *Main Street* and *Babbitt*, Lewis became a successful novelist and critic of American culture, winning the Nobel Prize for Literature in 1930. He returned frequently to Minnesota; never able to deny his underlying attachment to the Northern Middle West, he described it as "... the newest empire of the world ... a land of dairy herds and exquisite lakes, of new automobiles and tar-paper shanties and silos like red towers, of clumsy speech and a hope that is boundless." Lewis' talent declined and he died alone in Italy on January 10, 1951. As he had requested, his ashes were brought home to Sauk Centre.

ERECTED BY MINNESOTA HISTORICAL SOCIETY 1966

Sinclair Lewis' birthplace in Sauk Centre, Minnesota.

"The Can Pile" in Casselton, North Dakota.

Theodore Roosevelt National Park North Dakota.

Roxie II outside the Livingston Inn in Livingston, Montana.

The Space Needle. Seattle, Washington.

The closest I could get to a volcanic eruption.

The Oregon coast.

Judy locked in the van?

Paul Bunyon and Babe the Blue Ox outside "The Trees of Mystery" in Klamath, California.
(Note Kathy standing at Paul's right foot for scale.)

The tallest trees on earth. Redwood National and State Parks California.

California gas prices in 2004.

Roxie II in front of John Steinbeck's birthplace in Salinas, California.

John Steinbeck's final resting place in
The Garden of Memories Cemetery in Salinas, California.

Me shooting footage of the vineyards in central California.

Airplane graveyard. Mojave, California.

Vicki Cain

My Route 66 motel room.

Vicki Cain

A traditional Route 66 sight.

Old Town Albuquerque, New Mexico.

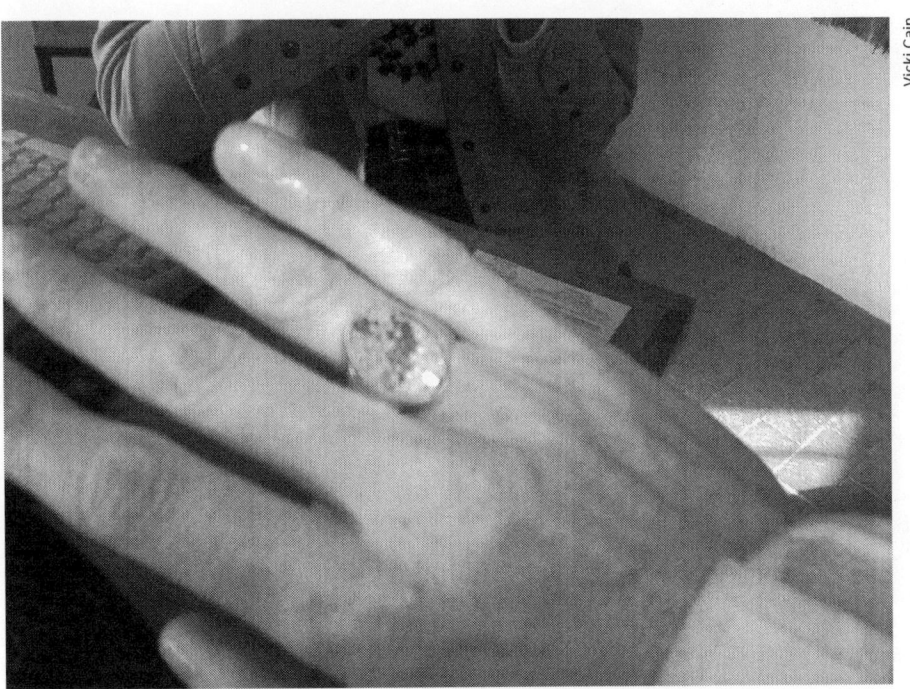

My lovely new turquoise ring.

On the Continental Divide wearing my new cowboy hat.

The Route 66 ghost town of Glenrio, New Mexico.

The Route 66 ghost town of Glenrio, Texas.

The Copper Caboose in Lubbuck, Texas.

A Texas-sized "small" beer.

Just outside of Baird, Texas.

Vicki Cain

Ruby Bridges and me.

Kathleen Cain Nastrom

All tuckered out.

Coeur d'Alene, Idaho, to Seattle, Washington
Thursday, October 7, 2004

The weather was beautiful in the morning, so I took my breakfast down to the lake to eat it alfresco. I sat down on a bench. Judy hopped up on the bench next to me and leaned her weight on my shoulder. That's one thing I never could get enough of—Judy's complete and utter love sluttiness. I put my arm around her and we sat and watched the birds. Suddenly, I heard a loud motor. Looking up, I saw a bright blue and white seaplane coming in for a landing right overhead! It was a perfect landing on the sparkling water, just a few dozen yards away. That clinched it. Lake Coeur d'Alene is definitely heaven with a little bit of magic thrown in, but I had to get moving. Today I would finally get to the Pacific Ocean, and thereby complete the first third of the journey. It was a milestone day, and I was eager to see an old friend in Seattle.

Compared to Montana, Idaho is a small state, and it seemed like no time before I left the magical mountains and mists of Idaho and found myself crossing into Washington. I have to say I was caught completely off guard at the landscape of eastern Washington. I had been to the Pacific Northwest once before, and I remembered the pine forests, moss-covered ground, beautiful mountains, and picturesque waterfalls. I thought the forests of Idaho just continued on to the coast. Boy, howdy, was I wrong.

Eastern Washington is a desert. Well, I'm not sure if it's technically a desert, but it's definitely more like southern California than Idaho. Eerie, moon-like landscape surrounded me for miles and miles. The sky was almost as huge as it was in Montana! The road curved alongside the Columbia River, and the desolate landscape resembled Tatooine in *Star*

Wars more than *Northern Exposure's* Cicely, Alaska. Just where the heck was I? It turns out I had entered volcano territory.

Between 17 and 6 million years ago, lava flowed from hundreds of volcanic eruptions in this area, and on its slow, molten journey toward the Pacific Ocean, it created a 63,000-square-mile plain—the Columbia Plateau. Running through the middle of this 6,000-foot-thick lava bed is the Columbia River, which supplies more water to the Pacific Ocean than any other river in North or South America. It was achingly beautiful in its starkness.

I finally found myself arriving on the outskirts of Seattle, just in time for rush hour. I was a free spirit blowing with the wind—had no schedule or responsibilities to anyone but myself—but for the rest of Seattle, it was a normal Thursday and time to go home. Seattle was also the first town since Minneapolis where I actually had dinner plans! I had arranged to meet my old friend, Ohio (yes, that's her name). I hadn't seen her in several years so we had a lot to catch up on. During the recession of the early 1990s, Ohio and I worked together at a copy store in Uptown, Minneapolis. She was writing her first novel at the time, and after several more novels, she eventually expanded into making films. On this trip I had been randomly shooting video of whatever I thought was interesting, but really didn't have a plan for how to put the thing together upon my return home. I was eager to pick her brain about how I should proceed. To be honest, I also was feeling a little overwhelmed and was needing a "buck up, kiddo" talk. I knew Ohio could dish one out like nobody's business. She didn't disappoint.

We got together at a dive-y restaurant that was loud and kitschy and fun and it took her no time at all to give me utter and complete perspective on my current predicament.

"Vicki, look at it this way...Ninety-nine percent of the people who have an idea for a film never get the script written. Ninety-nine percent of the people who get a script written never get to development. Ninety-nine percent of the people who get to development never get to production. So, the fact that you've gotten this far is more than most people ever do! You've won. Now shut up, drink a beer and let's celebrate."

She was right. She's always right. So, I shut up, drank a beer, and had a raucously good time swapping stories about times gone by with my old friend.

Late in the evening, I wandered back to Roxie II to get Judy and we headed back to our motel by the Space Needle. The Space Needle sure was pretty all lit up at night. It was built in 1962 for the World's Fair, and has since become one of the most recognized images of the Seattle skyline, yet to my knowledge, Steinbeck never saw it in person. I understand some locals find it ugly, annoying, trite, and all those other things that local people feel about tourist attractions in their town. As I walked toward the futuristic spaceship/restaurant that balanced on three spindly legs, I was mesmerized. How amazing it must have been to see when it opened in 1962, years before the space race was won. It must have been brilliant to see. And now, as it twinkled through the coastal foggy mist, it still seemed to represent the future and the excitement of the unknown.

Seattle, Washington, to Netarts, Oregon
Friday, October 8, 2004

As I checked out of my motel early in the morning, the clerk told me that since I was on "such a cool trip," Judy got to stay for free! Once again, I was amazed at how much more dog-friendly motels are outside of New England. However, it could have just been Judy's shameless flirting with the desk clerk. My God, that dog could charm a cat into giving her a tongue bath (as she did once).

My first stop in the morning was Seattle's Old Port to see if clams and fish and shrimp were still sold on ice in the open market. They were and then some. There was seafood and flowers and ice cream and everything you could possibly imagine in a market that catered largely to the tourist trade. It reminded me of the old Farmer's Market in Los Angeles, only with more of a coastal vibe. The fishermen were unloading their catch just outside the buildings and florists were unloading their blooms on the street side. I instantly felt overwhelmed by the number of options of things to buy so I promptly bought nothing. The aromas, the colors, and the sounds of the busy market were more than enough to take home with me. I was thrilled to see that the market hadn't changed one iota in 44 years, and I suspect it never will.

I thought about taking a drive around town, but I was very, very eager to get going. Over the past month, the news was reporting that Mount St. Helens was giving hints that it might be interested in blowing its top again in the very near future. Every day there were more reports regarding the imminent eruption. I was very excited to see the volcano, and possibly witness an eruption.

In 1960, Mount St. Helens was a dormant volcano at the edge of a picturesque lake in the middle of some of the loveliest woods on the western seaboard. No doubt, if the weather was clear, John Steinbeck and Charley saw it as well as Mount Rainier and Mount Hood as they drove southward. That all changed forever on May 18, 1980, when Mount St. Helens erupted, burning 230 acres of woodlands and dropping ash across 11 states. What was one of the most beautiful vacation spots in the upper Northwest was decimated in a matter of hours. Fifty-seven people lost their lives, including the first person to report the eruption, David A. Johnston, who was manning an observation post six miles from the crater, only to be swept away seconds later by the pyroclastic flow. In an ironic twist of fate, the day I left on my journey was the beginning of an active earthquake period on the mountain. On October 1 an ash plume was released from the volcano, and for the past week the entire area had been on volcano watch. I eagerly scurried down the road toward potential disaster.

As I got to the highway turnoff, signs were posted that only the furthest lookout station from the mountain was open to visitors due to the potential eruption. Drat. Oh well, I figured I'd at least get a quick glimpse of what was left of the volcano, buy a postcard and maybe a souvenir snow globe (full of ash swirling around a collapsed Mount St. Helens?), and then head to Netarts, Oregon, where an old friend was waiting dinner for me. Rain was pelting down in torrents, and driving was stressful. Finally I found the parking lot and ran quick-like-a-bunny across the pavement to the visitors' center. As soon as I entered the very lovely building, I realized I wasn't going to see any volcano that day. The viewing window was completely fogged over with the rain and clouds, and visibility was about ten feet. I cannot say that I've ever been more disappointed at a National Park than I was at that moment. Sure, it was too dangerous to go closer, and there is only so much you can see from several miles away, but I guess I sort of hoped there'd be a volcano-cam being live-streamed from a camera mounted on a tree nearer the summit or something. To be fair, though, the park ranger was extremely knowledgeable and apologetic for the horrendous weather conditions, and yet...wait...was that a really awesome gift shop? Oh Ho HO!!! I found the justification for my detour! Surprisingly, they were selling a lot of items commemorating the Lewis and Clark Expedition. Holy cow! I'd completely forgotten about those guys.

As it turned out, 2004 was the 200th anniversary of the launch of the Lewis and Clark Expedition. Those wacky, 19th century guys who spent two years traveling across this great country, collecting knowledge about the resources America had just received from the Louisiana Purchase. They didn't find the Northwest Passage to Asia, but they did get to the Pacific Ocean and back, and only one person died on the journey—Sgt. Charles Floyd—of acute appendicitis.

I commemorated those daring young men with the purchase of a new wooden replica of the compass just like the one they used to navigate across the entire country. I figured if the rain and fog continued, it actually might come in handy on this trip, and if it was good enough to get Lewis and Clark to the Pacific Ocean and back, well, then by golly, it was good enough to get me to a highway. And so I left the lame, non-erupting volcano behind.

Driving in rain is exhausting. Even though I drove less time on this day than any day previously, I found myself completely drained and spent by dinnertime. Maybe it was because I knew I would be seeing my old friend, Ann, who was putting me up for the night. I knew there was going to be hot food, good wine, and a soft bed just waiting for me. Ann moved to coastal Oregon a year or two before to teach school, and knew a friend in the area who got her started in the Tillimook school district. Ann had an apartment with a view of the Pacific Ocean, and she was paying around $500 a month rent. I was shocked at her luck until I entered Netarts. It's a lovely little village, but it was a little village pretty much in the middle of a big bad forest. Calling the area rural was an understatement. As Ann mentioned to me once, the nearest Target store was an hour away. Even in the small town in Nebraska that I grew up in, there was a Kmart and a McDonalds. Not so with Netarts. However, for scenery, it was breathtaking. Even with the clouds and rain, the ocean was alive and vibrant. As we sat on her porch overlooking the ocean and smelling the salt water, I couldn't believe this was such a sparsely populated area. It should be a National Park! Then again, if anyone else found out about Netarts, Ann wouldn't have this amazing view for only $500 a month.

Girl talk ensued. Wine was drunk. The world's problems were solved. A good sleep was had.

Netarts, Oregon, to Crescent City, California
Saturday, October 9, 2004

After morning coffee on the porch overlooking the Pacific Ocean (did I mention the amazing view?) I bid Ann goodbye, took Judy on a quick jaunt along the beach, and once again headed south. I was very excited to get to the Redwoods.

I drove along the very scenic highway that hugged the coastline. The rain had let up a bit, so the drive was much more pleasant with the sunrise. There were still extremely active clouds in the sky that gave the scenery added passion. At one overlook, I stumbled upon a large bunch of kite-flyers. Vividly colored kites of all shapes and sizes danced and swirled in the mighty wind as the waves crashed onto shore underneath them. All it was lacking was a musical score.

But what does all this have to do with politics, you ask?

Nineteen-sixty, the year of Steinbeck's trip, was an election year, and the candidates were John F. Kennedy and Richard M. Nixon. With the Cold War, the Vietnam War, and the Space Race, it was a very pivotal election. John F. Kennedy ended up winning in one of the closest elections ever.

The election of 2004 was between republican President George W. Bush and democrat Senator John Kerry. This was the first election since the September 11, 2001, terrorist attacks on the World Trade Center. The country had gotten more and more polarized over the subsequent three years.

As I drove through Florence, Oregon, I noticed a group of a dozen or so political protesters. I pulled over to hear what they had to say. Assuming it was a group of democrats, since I don't normally see republicans out street-side carrying hand-lettered signs protesting, I expected to hear a lot of liberal, pro-Kerry discourse.

The first sign I saw said:

> Bush→
> ←Truth

I was on the right track with my assumption.

After introducing myself to the gentleman with the sign, and telling him about the purpose of my trip, he completely floored me by skipping the political rant and exclaiming, "I love John Steinbeck!" Then he proceeded to extrapolate on the value and meaning of *The Grapes of Wrath* and *In Dubious Battle* and how it still pertains to our daily lives at the dawn of the 21st Century. His fellow protesters came around and jumped into the conversation. I soon found out that the only thing these people had in common was their desire to see John Kerry in the White House. One gentleman was a Vietnam War veteran who, after being decorated for valor, was now a pacifist. A woman holding a sign that said "Save the children" was a mother and a teacher who lived in the suburbs. Another man was what I would call a more stereotypical aging hippie—a man in his 50s wearing tie-dye. As diverse as they all were, they all had a story or opinion to add about their favorite John Steinbeck book. It was very entertaining, but I didn't really learn that much about politics.

Judy hopped out and said a brief hello to our new friends, and we left the gaggle of political protesters with a warm feeling in our hearts. We still had no idea where the current election might lead us. Regardless of background, religion, or political persuasion, literature is a universal unifier. Maybe politicians should spend less time talking and more time reading?

Just sayin'.

* * * * *

Later that night, through a dumb fluke, I was locked in the back of the van in a parking lot in Crescent City, California. I huddled in the dark interior of the large blue steel can and pondered my options. Sitting in the cramped space in the dark, it was hard to believe that just moments ago, I was actually relieved to be done traveling for the day and was looking forward to a relaxing dinner.

I looked out the window and saw the pulsing light from a neon sign slash through the coal-black northern California night. Only one person knew where I was, but she had no idea I was trapped. If only I could get a message to her.

Suddenly I remembered my cell phone. For once I actually had it with me in a time of emergency; however, as the past 10 days had taught me, the odds of having cell reception were 50/50 at best.

I turned it on and held my breath while I waited to see if I was within range of a cell tower. After a few breathless moments, I was rewarded with the comforting glow of three solid bars. Hurrah!

Hurriedly scrolling through my saved phone numbers, I was looking for "Kathy Cell" so I could call my dear and beloved sister. For whom I'd never felt more affection, never said a cross word about, and who was at that very moment just across the parking lot in the warm restaurant waiting for me, while unbeknownst to her, I was frantic for release from the cold metal prison. As I dialed, I glanced into the cab of the van through the metal gate that held me captive, and my gaze zoomed in slow-motion towards the cell phone that rested quietly on the dash—just like in a bad horror movie. In that instant, the harsh reality hit me that

Kathy hadn't taken her phone with her into the cheerful restaurant. After all, why would she? She hadn't had any cell reception since Seattle. For a moment I imagined I was in a real-life horror movie and any minute now, zombies were going to start approaching the van and I would be one of those characters that would utter, "Hello? Is someone out there?" just before being zombified.

My heart sank as my horror-movie fantasy dissipated, and I settled back into the darkness. Suddenly, I felt a cold nose bump my arm. Judy was now done with her dinner and wanted some attention. She leaned onto my chest and stretched her nose up toward mine, then gave a small burp in my face. I put my arm around her and felt instantly better, but secretly was embarrassed at our current predicament. How long had it been since I stepped into the back of the van to feed her, and the door blew shut behind me and locked? Ten minutes? An hour? Two? What a dumb time to realize I should have signed up for AAA.

And yet, I did have one small hope for rescue before I starved to death and buzzards started circling the van. My cell phone was still active.

My mind scurried to figure out a way to get a message to Kathy, for therein lay my salvation. In a burst of genius, I realized I could call my mother in Iowa, have her call directory assistance to get the restaurant's phone number, and then call and have them get Kathy the message that I was locked in the vehicle. Of course! Gosh it's great to live in an era of technology! Once again my hopes were lifted as I hurriedly dialed the phone.

"Hello, Mom?" I said.

"Hi! Where are you now?"

"Look, Mom. I've got a bit of an emergency. I'm locked in the back of the van with Judy at this restaurant in Crescent City, California. Kathy is already inside at a table waiting for me. Could you find the phone number for the restaurant, call them, and have them send her out to spring me?"

"You're locked in the van?"

There was a brief pause as this information sunk into her head, and I waited for her to jump into action and call the National Guard to rescue her youngest offspring from certain death.

Suddenly, an explosion of laughter burst out of the phone, and I had to remove it from my ear. I have to admit I completely realized the ridiculousness of the situation, but I wasn't prepared for my own mother to be laughing at me while I was still deep in the throes of the crisis. I figured the laughter would come later once I was safely ensconced in the restaurant with a plate of meatloaf in front of me, away from the dangers of vagrant lock-picking thieves, rapists, and murderers who no doubt were patrolling the area around the van at that moment.

"Hahahaha," was still coming out of the phone.

"Mom—" I began.

"Hahaha... KENNY! Vicki's locked herself in the van! Hahahahaha."

"Mom, I need—"

"Hahahaha. Oh boy, that's a good one! Hahahaha."

"Mom...could you put Dad on the phone?"

"Ha ha ha ha."

"MOM!"

"Oh, sorry. Hehe. What is it you want me to do? Hahaha. [To my dad] YES! SHE LOCKED HERSELF IN THE VAN IN A PARKING LOT. WHY DON'T YOU EVER LISTEN TO ME?"

"MOM. Could you please find the phone number and have Kathy come out and release me? PLEASE? I'm starting to lose weight from lack of eating and if I starve to death, there won't be much of me left for Judy to chew on to sustain herself."

"OK, ok. Give me a minute. Hahahahaha. I'll call you back." Click.

I hung up the phone and waited.

Five minutes later, I was still waiting. My eyes fervently scanned the parking lot searching for some safe-looking passersby who might be un-afraid to approach a crazy woman in the back of a large panel van, and yet I figured whoever would be brave enough to do that, might also be looking to bum a ride somewhere, or expect a free meal, or just simply want to ravage the helpless crazy woman.

Five minutes even later, I was losing the feeling in my legs, so I shifted them out from under me and sat in an equally uncomfortable position on the metal floor. Just what was taking so long? Since there had still been no news from my mother, and my sister hadn't come running out of the building, I called my mother to see what was up.

"Hahahaha...Yes?" she said.

"Well? Have you called the restaurant?" I asked.

"Hahahaha. Oh, no, not yet. I'm not done laughing! Hahaha. Er...what was the name of the restaurant again?"

I couldn't believe it.

They say just before you die, your entire life flashes before you. I am now a staunch believer in this theory, since once it became obvious that my salvation wouldn't be appearing very soon, the entire past year flashed before my eyes. All the feelings I had managed to keep at bay suddenly flooded upon me in an instant and overran the optimism I had somehow managed to cling to at each low point. The endless anxiety, the doubts and fears, and most of all, the tide of overwhelming obstacles that threatened to drown my grandiose plans came crashing down upon me. In the back of that blue van on that dark night, for the first time since this crazy project had started, I was left submerged in a pool of depression and wondered what to do.

God, I was such an idiot.

I felt the tears well up from deep inside my eyes and everything blurred as I looked down at Judy through the lake of sadness that engulfed me. She looked at me with pity in her eyes, and licked my nose to comfort me. I hugged her close and pledged that I was not going to cry. No, I wasn't. Eventually Mom would stop laughing and call the restaurant and Kathy would spring me. At least I hoped so.

"What the heck's keeping you?" a familiar voice boomed from outside the van. Dear Lord Almighty! It was Kathy!! She'd come to rescue me! I knew Mom would pull through!

"Did Mom finally call you?"

"Huh? No. I just got tired of waiting for you and decided to come out here and see what was up."

So Mom was probably still laughing. I should have called my dad. It reminds me of the time my parents moved and didn't give me their new phone number, but they gave it to Kathy. I always knew she was their favorite.

But all that was now behind me. I listened to Kathy laughing at me all the way back into the restaurant. I knew that this story would be repeated at holiday gatherings for the rest of my life, and throughout the generations, as a new page in the book of family lore along with the story of my great-grandmother who drank her own urine out on the prairie as a cure for croup while she traveled via covered wagon to her homestead in western Nebraska circa. 1890. I didn't care. I was free.

Crescent City, California, to Menlo Park, California
Sunday, October 10, 2004

That night we stayed in one of the scariest motels I've ever been in. It was cheap and clean, but it hadn't been remodeled in any way since 1960—the furniture was Danish Modern. The place had the seedy feel of a hideout for murderers, or possibly even a place where murders take place once in a while. The door did have a deadbolt lock, which made me feel better, but I still felt the need to move a chair under the doorknob— just in case some mobsters or drug dealers wanted to borrow the room during the night. The electrical outlets were seriously sub-code—the non-grounded outlets were only two-pronged. I wasn't able to charge my video camera or my phone. The only bright point was when we woke up in the morning, Kathy was in such a hurry to get out of the creepy motel that she completely loaded the van all by herself by the time I finished my shower. I don't think I'd ever seen her move that fast and furious before or since. Thanks to Kathy's Herculean efforts, we were back on the road by 8:00 a.m.

The Redwoods were just down the road apiece, and since we had hurried out of the scary motel so quickly we needed sustenance. We stopped at the Forest Café restaurant just across the street from a 30-foot fiberglass sculpture of Paul Bunyan and Babe the Blue Ox, The mythic pair were located in the parking lot of the Trees of Mystery, a tourist trap of wondrous proportions. Who cares that there were natural, 100-foot-high trees surrounding me with their majestic glory? There was a tourist gift shop across the street! I'm such a sucker for anything kitschy and larger-than-life. I hadn't seen anything this exciting since the Wisconsin Dells.

After snarfing down my scrambled eggs, I practically ran across the street to solve the mystery of the trees and pick up some tchotchkes in the process. Unfortunately, we just missed the next tour for the Trees of Mystery and we weren't able to wait around for the next one, so I am sure we severely missed out on something great; but the gift shop was amazing. It had shot glasses, back scratchers, boxes, key rings, mirrors, mugs, pens, magnets, and everything else you could think of made out of redwood. I have to admit I was first a bit taken aback when I thought of all the trees that were destroyed for this glorious display of consumerism. I was informed that the Redwoods are not an endangered species of tree. There is even a motel down the road that is made entirely of redwood. After the better part of a half hour, I found myself handing over quite a bit of money to the lady at the cash register, when she randomly volunteered, "Would you like to see some elk?"

Real, live elk?

"Just go down the road into the park. After you cross the bridge, take your third left. Then follow that road past the old farm stand. When you get to the jig in the road, you'll want to go to the right, but don't. Follow around the lake instead for about three-quarters of a mile, then take the second right, drive through the tree, and you should see some around there."

She lost me somewhere just before the lake, but I believe I enthused greatly enough to convince her I committed that all to memory, and thanked her for the tip. There really was no way I was going to go chasing after a herd of elk that may or may not be wandering around near a tree you can drive through, even though I've always wanted to do that. Besides, I was pretty sure Roxie was too big to fit through the tree. Nevertheless, as I crossed the bridge, I found myself trying to remember what her directions were. Was it left after the bridge or right...when suddenly there they were! Six elk were hanging out in the front yard of a house on the left side of the road I was on! Holy Smokes (BBQ)!

I spun Roxie around in a move that would have made Jim Rockford proud and which threw Judy over in her seat and Kathy into the back, then before the dust settled, I quietly inched up as close to the elk as I could. I guess I hadn't thought about what an elk really looks like. I think I was expecting them to look like really big deer, but they are much, much sturdier than that. They had beefy shoulders and huge antlers and their heads looked like they were part moose. They also didn't seem the least bit frightened of me. I guess if I was that big with six feet of weaponry attached to my forehead, I wouldn't be scared of much, either. More cars pulled over to gawk at wildlife in its natural habitat—the Johnsons' (it was the name on the mailbox) driveway. I grabbed the video camera and prayed that there was enough battery power to capture my American adventure safari. I felt it wise to not actually get out of the van, so I rolled the window down and pulled myself through it, sat my rump on the windowsill and tried to zoom close enough so when I showed this to people, they'd think I was standing right next to them. I managed to get about a minute's worth of footage before the mini-cam went dark. But boy, was I thrilled. Surprisingly, Judy was unfazed. The dog has a conniption fit when a bicycle passes by our house, but when there is a thousand-pound Cervidae standing in front of her, she couldn't care less. Dogs are weird.

Since my camera was now kaput for the day, there really was no reason to dawdle with the elk any longer, so I backed up the van and headed deep into the Redwood forest.

Steinbeck had been to the Redwoods prior to his trip with Charley, and he had some interesting stories to tell about it, but he, too, was mostly excited to see how Charley would react to seeing such huge trees. He logically suspected that Charley would be dumbfounded, awed, or excited at the sight of them. Charley, however, couldn't have cared less. He just did his normal business as if he was walking around his backyard. Steinbeck tried to get Charley to look up and see the tremendous height of these phenomenal freaks of nature, but to no avail. Considering Judy's lack of interest at the elk, I wondered if she would give a crap about big trees.

I was surprised at how difficult it was to drive through the Redwoods. The sun was shining brightly, but since the trees were so tall, the light didn't reach the ground in most places. As I drove along, slashes of bright light would flicker over my windshield every few seconds, which made driving as difficult as driving into a strobe light. I finally pulled over in a quiet and relatively secluded area and eagerly jumped out with Judy. Would she perk up her ear, arch up her tail, and sniff the air excitedly? Or would she just put her nose to the ground and do nothing out of the ordinary? Although she was very peppy to be out of the van, she did more of the latter than the former. She was more interested in the smells the forest provided than the height of the trees. Maybe their beauty is truly only appreciated by humans?

After sniffing around a bit, we headed back south down the long and winding road. The flashes of light reflecting off my windshield caused me massive amounts of stress, and by the time we got to San Francisco, I was completely wiped out. All I really wanted to do was to find a motel, eat a large dinner, and collapse. However, I once again had plans to meet friends for the evening. Within a few minutes of arriving at Lisa and Nik's, however, I immediately felt better. It was very good to relax with old friends and marvel at how much their daughter (whom they named after my cat) had grown since I'd last seen her. Judy was just fine waiting in the van for a while.

Menlo Park, California, to Tulare, California
Monday, October 11, 2004

In the morning, Lisa met me for breakfast. Since my motel didn't offer any sort of Internet connection, she took me to the local library so I could update my blog before getting back on the road. She signed me into a computer and bid me farewell while she headed off to work. Before I wrote down my travails of the past few days, I checked the news and discovered that Christopher Reeve had died the day before.

Initially, I found it difficult to understand why this felt like such a huge blow to me. Christopher Reeve will always be Superman to me. I also loved him in *Deathtrap, Somewhere in Time,* and his Maidenform underwear commercials in the mid-1980s made me swoon. The premature deaths of many movie stars I held in higher regard didn't hit me as hard as his did. I think it's because after the tragic horsing accident that left him a quadriplegic, he became one of the most inspiring human beings alive. He championed the advancement of spinal column research and treatment for the rest of his life, and just months before he died, he had moved his legs for the first time since the accident. When I saw that, I cried with joy along with the rest of the world. At that moment I knew he was going to beat the astronomical odds and walk again. He believed in conquering the impossible and he made me believe it, too. His perseverance and guts gave us all hope. Now he was gone before he could save the world. I wasn't mourning the loss of a movie star. I was mourning the loss of a great man. Superman was human, after all.

And so, with a sad heart, I got back on the road. Today was the day I visited Steinbeck's home—Salinas, California.

John Steinbeck's hometown had turned against him when he wrote *The Grapes of Wrath* because they felt he hadn't painted them in a positive light. He eventually left Salinas for good and settled into his life on the East Coast. His friends were there, sure, but in his mind, things and people had somewhat froze in time when he left. Upon his return in 1960, the hole he left when he vacated had been filled with other people, other stories, other lives. Rather than finding the ghosts he remembered from times gone by, he realized he was the ghost—a mere fragment of who he once was. He left town saddened and wizened. He was to return one more time, and this time he stayed for good. Salinas is not only John Steinbeck's birthplace, but also his final resting place.

When I arrived in town, it was obvious that whatever ill feelings the town had toward John Steinbeck, they had gotten over it. In 2004 he was a hero. His home is now a museum and café, they've named a library after him, and the impressive National Steinbeck Center shimmers at the end of Main Street. It was to be my first stop.

The National Steinbeck Center opened its doors in 1998 and serves not only as a museum to the man and his works, but also as an educational center for agriculture in central California. They have exhibits commemorating each of Steinbeck's books, movies, and stories; and they also fund a scholarship for promising writers. Before I started my trip, I had contacted the center in the hopes I might get some more information about Steinbeck's trip (a map would have been nice, but no), and they gave me lots of information on how to research my journey. Overall, I felt very indebted to the center and to their helpful staff. I spent my first few minutes there speaking with the employees and volunteers. Everyone seemed to be thrilled to hear that I was recreating this journey, and as Steinbeck himself stated, they all wished they could go along with me. They even gave me directions to his gravesite.

I then entered the museum proper.

I was nervous. There was one thing in particular that I was desperate to see. Something that I had a clear vision of in my mind even though I'd never laid eyes on it. I was afraid that when I did see it, the reality of it wouldn't meet the expectations of my imagination...the original Rocinante.

After Steinbeck's trip, the truck had been sold to Mr. William Plate. When the center opened in the 1990s, the Plates generously donated it to the museum, where it was restored to its original glory. I was eager to see this vehicle that had been such a large part of my many late night readings and fantasies of doing exactly what I had been doing for the past two weeks. Each corner I turned around, I expected to see the green Ford truck staring back at me, but each time I was disappointed. I tried to sit through some of the educational films about *The Red Pony* or *The Grapes of Wrath*, but my mind was clearly elsewhere. I was also worried about Judy.

The temperature that day was nearly 100 degrees Fahrenheit. Roxie II was parked under a teeny-tiny tree that barely cast a shadow on the windshield, and Judy was locked inside her. Thanks to blasting the air-conditioning all morning, when I left the van, the temperature inside it was very comfortable. However, I knew it would heat up quickly in the sweltering midday sun, so I knew I only had a few minutes before I'd have to go back to the van to run the air-conditioner again to guarantee Judy wouldn't overheat.

I guess I had anticipated some sort of angel chorus to burst into song when I first laid eyes on the 1960 pickup, but there was none. It wasn't the magical moment I was hoping for as I slowly turned one final corner, and there she was...Rocinante in all her glory, exactly how I pictured her. Really. Exactly. It was almost surreal to not see any glaring differences from my fantasy version, but there were none. It felt weird.

When I was 12 years old, my family went to Philadelphia on vacation. When we visited Philadelphia Hall and stood in the same room that the Declaration of Independence was signed, I remember being told that the floor was the original floor, and I couldn't stop staring at it. As the docent rambled on about the spectacular building and all the historical events that those walls had witnessed, all I could think was, "I'm standing on the same floor that George Washington, Thomas Jefferson, and Benjamin Franklin stood on. At some point they probably stepped on this board. Even if they didn't, they certainly laid eyes on it. And now I'm here. Standing on this board." It positively blew my mind.

I had a similar experience the first time I went to Fenway Park. I was 18 years old, just graduated from high school, and my parents had given me a trip to Massachusetts to visit my cousin. My uncle took us to a Red Sox game one afternoon. I knew the park was the oldest baseball stadium in the country, but I wasn't prepared for the feeling I got from the wooden seats. I was instantly connected to an earlier time when there were no night games and the players wore knickers. As I gazed over the beautiful park, I could imagine all the millions of people who had sat in this seat before me. The names of the players were different, but the field was the same. After hitting his famous 1946, 502-foot home run, did Ted Williams gaze across this very seat I was sitting in now? Who was sitting here on a day when Babe Ruth struck out? Even the day I attended, I witnessed a monumental event when Carl "Yaz" Yastrzemski dropped his glove after the pitch and still managed to catch a third-out foul ball in his bare hands. All these events spanned decades, but in a moment, they became one via the tangible connection of the seat my butt was comfortably settled into.

I expected to experience a similar wrinkle-in-time feeling when I saw Rocinante, but I did not. It just looked like a truck that my grandfather might have owned. Maybe it was because the truck wasn't accessible in a physical sense. It was safely secured behind Plexiglas in order to preserve it for future generations (as it should), but I desperately wanted the physical connection. It was time to visit the man himself.

I started by going to his birthplace, which was located only a few blocks away. It was now a café and restaurant that was open to the public, and I was hoping to have lunch there. As I arrived at the very lovely Victorian home at 132 Central Avenue, I managed to get a parking spot right in front! I couldn't believe my luck. I parked and quickly ran up the front steps and found a sign, "Closed on Mondays." Wha? Drat. So much for my lunch in Steinbeck's living room.

I next drove across town to the Garden of Memories Cemetery and slowly drove down the leaf-strewn drive in the bright sunshine. As we crept along, Judy seemed almost as excited as I was, but we both were quiet. The moment demanded solemnity and reverence. What is it about cemeteries? For being a place of death, they are tremendously warm and welcoming. Perhaps it's our subconscious knowledge that one day we will be resting there forever. Or maybe it's just that they are designed to comfort the living. Either way, this cemetery was no less pleasant than any other I've ever been to, and better than some.

I squinted at the tombstones to try to find the name "Hamilton," which is the name of his wife's family's plot where he is buried. Judy barked at a squirrel or something, so I looked up and there was a sign in front of me, about six feet high, that said:

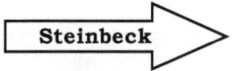

Apparently, I wasn't the first person to make this pilgrimage.

I parked by the sign, left Judy inside with the cool air-conditioning, and made the rest of the journey by foot. It wasn't far, just a dozen steps or so from the road. And then there he was. John Steinbeck.

Other people had been there before me and placed candles, flowers, and the like in memoriam. I hadn't had any forethought of that type, and to be honest, I hadn't really known what to expect from this visitation. I was surprisingly sad. After all, this was someone I'd never met, who died when I was only four years old, and yet he had inspired me to follow my dreams, step outside my comfort zone, and attempt the largest challenge of my life. I was currently standing in 100-degree heat 3,000 miles from home and it was all his fault.

I stayed a few minutes and paid my respects to one of the greatest American writers of all time, and felt completely and truly humbled. I felt a bit sheepish, too, like I was a little kid shyly waiting to be introduced to their childhood hero. How amazing that even their death doesn't stop us from worshipping our heroes. In a lot of ways, I was glad that John Steinbeck was dead. I never could have met him in person without either speaking gibberish or making a full-on jerk of myself, so it's probably best that our meeting was one-sided.

I felt the sweat dribble down my neck as I walked back to the van, and saw Judy's eyes following me from the passenger seat with her ear perked up, and a big smile upon her cute face. It was obvious that she was sitting comfortably in a controlled environment and for a second I laughed. I couldn't help it. She just is so silly sometimes and it's usually times when she's doing nothing unusual at all, like then.

Our next stop was one of great interest to me, because it was a tangible place that Steinbeck visited on his trip, and one that was very dear to his heart. When Steinbeck visited Monterey, he visited his friend, Joe Garcia, at Joe's bar. This event was so pivotal because it was the time that he realized that even though the place and the people were the same as they were years ago, he was no longer a part of it. This fascinated me, and I wanted to see the bar where he had this epiphany. I was told the building that had once housed Joe Garcia's bar was now an historical site—The First Brick House in Monterey.

Let's just say that finding The First Brick House in Monterey is much more difficult than it sounds. You'd think a landmark such as THE FIRST BRICK HOUSE IN MONTEREY would be rather easy to find, especially when the Monterey Tourist Office had a map with it very clearly marked— just south of the Monterey wharf, and smack dab in the middle of Historic Monterey. However, as Judy and I walked up one street and down the next, I couldn't find the street that was marked so clearly on the map. I saw coffee shops and boutiques and classrooms for the Brandman University, but I couldn't find this tourist spot. There was no signage anywhere to even hint that I was on the right track. Finally, after wandering around like a chicken with my head cut off, I decided to take a load off. I headed onto the college campus where I saw some benches next to a fountain where I could rest. After I passed a couple buildings, I noticed a brick structure on my left, hidden deep in the campus. I had finally found it! I was confused as I looked more closely at the building. This didn't look like it was ever a bar, or even a public building. Granted, its location was odd, but who knows what the area was like in 1960? I have no idea if the college was there at the time. I figured the college bought the land at some point after 1960, and built the classrooms around the house since they couldn't tear it down due to the historical significance.

I still felt disappointed. The house looked like a large toolshed, or maybe an old goat barn. Other than the small plaque mounted on a stick in front of it, there was no signage of any sort. Try as I might I just couldn't imagine John Steinbeck visiting his colorful and passionate friends here. Nope. I just couldn't see it. Maybe I was incorrectly informed about the place? Maybe the true Joe Garcia's bar was in a different place altogether, and it had been torn down long ago? Maybe time had just finally blown away the nostalgic memories of a ghost who could never go home again?

It was starting to get dark, and I was starting to feel haunted by a life that I never knew. It was time to leave John Steinbeck's past behind and move on. After a quick dinner complete with pie (!) to perk myself up, I headed inland. Prior to this trip, most of my driving in California had been either the east/west route between Vegas and Los Angeles, or the north/south route between San Francisco and San Diego. Of the latter, at different journeys I'd taken the Pacific Coast Highway, Route 101, and Interstate 5. Rather than follow the coast, Steinbeck elected to turn inland instead, and I was eager to check out central California for the first time. I spent the next few hours gazing upon mile after mile of agriculture. Fruit orchards, vineyards, and even cotton fields (who knew?) slipped past my window. It was an amazingly abundant region.

I wanted to stop for the night near Fresno, but every motel that had a vacancy for miles around was insanely expensive. One place even wanted a $50 cash deposit for Judy! Fifty dollars?! That was the deposit that apartments ask for with a lease, for crying out loud! Needless to say, I didn't stay there. I also didn't stay in any of the other places I stopped at over the next two hours. Finally, I found a clean, affordable motel room in Tulare. I love Tulare.

Tulare, California, to Kingman, Arizona
Tuesday, October 12, 2004

I awoke to more heat and sunshine. Judy seemed unfazed. Considering how thick her undercoat was, I was completely caught by surprise
that I was more uncomfortable than she was. Maybe the thick fur keeps
her cool? Or maybe she's just one of those women who always look cool,
calm and collected. I've always wanted to be one of them—you know, the
women in those old photographs. Proper 19th century English ladies on
camels in the Sahara Desert wearing long dresses, petticoats, hats, and
gloves, yet somehow they don't have underarm sweat marks? I think
Judy was one of them in a past life. Lord knows I wasn't. It was only 8:00
a.m. and I was sweating buckets.

But, we were finally on our way to the Mojave Desert! I'm not sure exactly where it officially begins or ends, but we were driving right through
the middle of it, and our first stop was the airplane graveyard outside the
city of Mojave, California.

When I lived in Los Angeles, oh, so many years ago, my friend, Steve,
always wanted to take a drive to the airplane graveyard. We'd sit for
hours on his balcony and watch the planes cross the sky on their way to
LAX and the Van Nuys airport, and he was able to identify the planes as
they flew over.

"That's a DC-9," he'd say. "You can tell by the tail." I'd believe him,
most likely because I had no way of knowing whether he was right or
not, and also because we were usually imbibing a cold brew or two at
the time. It's generally wise not to hold someone to something they say
when they're drinking. We'd talk about planes and airports. He told me

that there was an airplane graveyard in the middle of the desert that the public could go visit. As a private pilot myself, I was mesmerized by the idea of old WWII and historic planes permanently grounded out in the middle of a dusty field—just waiting for people such as myself to arrive and climb aboard. B-17 Flying Fortresses. B-52 bombers. Corsairs, Swoose Gooses, and Black Widows. How much fun would it be to go visit these war machines and imagine the heroes who used to fly them? Steve and I made a pact and tipped another glass. One day soon we'd go. As is usually the case in these situations, all our grand plans to one day take a road trip to the Mojave Desert to visit the airplane graveyard ultimately never came to fruition.

And so, with warm reminiscences of Steve and realizing that one of our thrilling balcony adventures was about to come true, I followed signs to the Mojave Air and Space Port and eagerly drove up to the field that had mile after mile of commercial airplanes parked in rows like a parking lot.

What the...??

United, Delta, Northwest, Southwest, American, and all other airlines I could think of sat lined up in front of me. I drove further down the road, completely not believing my eyes, looking for the military planes of my dreams, but it was just one commercial plane after another. I was completely disappointed and crushed. And my lord, was it hot.

There was no explaining my next behavior. I welled up with rage and let fly a hissy fit of epic proportions. I swore up and down, threw my map across the front seat, shoved Judy away (she was trying to kiss me and make it better), and eventually stopped my tantrum just short of tears. In hindsight, my outburst was merely foreshadowing my inevitable road-fatigue breakdown, but at the time I felt I was completely justified by being cheated out of my dream of seeing a B-52 bomber.

Dejected, I resolved to get the heck out of California, so I squealed out of Mojave with a trail of dust behind me and headed into the desert with the destination of Kingman, Arizona.

The Mojave Desert stretches for 25,000 square miles. It was hosts the lowest and hottest place in North America, Death Valley. Its boundaries are defined by the Tehachapi, the San Gabriel and the San Bernadino mountain ranges. It's huge, it's hot, and it has Joshua trees.

I've heard of many people who don't understand the awesome beauty of the desert. I've always assumed that they have just never been there because it's one of the most fascinating and beautiful places on earth. The sky is so large you feel like a speck of dust in the wind. There is a tremendous comfort in feeling your own insignificance. As the sun sets, the colors of the landscape soften and God's paint box spills over everything in view. Mesas turn from dusty hills into jewel-covered, magical mountains. Scrubby flatland with threatening cacti becomes a warm orange carpet dotted with majestic silhouettes of the caretakers of the desert. The sky changes its mood by the second and allows you a peek into what heaven must look like. It's absolutely captivating. I was enraptured with the stunning and constantly changing vistas. I felt my anger and disappointment lift as the miles sped past me. The beauteous colors of the desert night lingered with me long after the sky turned black and thousands of diamonds sparkled in the sky. By the time I reached Kingman, I was relaxed and stopped at a small, but adorable Route 66 motor inn. In the morning, I would get my kicks, but tonight I would sleep.

Kingman, Arizona, to Albuquerque, New Mexico
Wednesday, October 13, 2004

I woke up rested and hitched up Judy to the leash for her morning constitutional. I opened the door and once my eyes adjusted to the brilliant sunshine, I fell back into the room stunned with the world around me. How on earth could I have not seen this sight when I arrived?

Bright red earth swept from my feet to the horizon. Beautiful large rocks were everywhere. In fact, once I got over the shock of the colors spread before me, I realized there really wasn't any place for Judy to relieve herself. Most dogs will go pretty much anywhere—on a tree, near a bush, in your shoe in your closet when they're mad at you—but Judy has always been very high-maintenance in this particular. When we lived in an apartment in L.A., we didn't have a yard, so we'd walk around the neighborhood several times a day. No matter how badly she needed to go, she would only go on some sort of vegetation. If we were crossing a large parking lot, she would find a lone dandelion growing up through a crack in the cement and water it. Therefore, when I looked around the motel and didn't even see a cactus in sight, I had a slight panic.

We ran across the parking lot to the rocky area that seemed to be the best chance for her to find something to her liking. Luckily, on the other side of the rocks was a sandier area where several scrubs were growing. Hooray. Judy took her time, though, and sniffed for quite a while before claiming her first part of Arizona. Once she baptized it, she owned it.

Upon my return to the motel, I noticed several of the rooms had small, white signs on the doors. In fact, there was one on my door. I guess I was so tired when I arrived the night before that I missed it.

"Martin Milner stayed here," it proudly proclaimed. Really? How very cool, and how very appropriate. I remember watching Martin Milner in *Adam 12* (when I was young I had a huge crush on his character's cohort, Jim Reed) and I also loved him as the "two-bit banjo player...with a mouth as big as a basket and twice as empty," Steve Dallas in the incredibly awesome Tony Curtis and Burt Lancaster movie, *The Sweet Smell of Success*. However, I know most people probably remember him for his 1950s television role as Tod Stiles in *Route 66*, which was about two guys in a Corvette traveling America. Obviously, since this motel was on Route 66, no doubt Mr. Milner's connection to that TV series was why this room was dedicated to him.

The room next to mine had a sign, too.

"Ronald McDonald stayed here." Dang. That was even cooler. As much as I liked the fact that Pete Malloy and I used the same shower, it would have been much more fun to be able to tell people I shared a bed with Ronald McDonald.

After finishing waking up for the day, I headed into the motel lobby to settle up my bill. I was hot on my quest of finding a cowboy hat. Gosh darn it, I'd been looking at every gin joint and brothel from Butte, Montana, to Kingman, Arizona, and so far I'd found nothing. I decided that day to also find myself a genuine turquoise ring. I figured if I couldn't find it on Route 66, I couldn't find it anywhere. The motel lobby was done up in a very kitschy 1950s style with lots of Coca-Cola posters and Elvis memorabilia. Even the lady at the front desk had a big smile on her face just like Mrs. Cunningham always did in *Happy Days*. I decided she looked honest enough. If she couldn't point me in the direction of some western wear, I seriously wondered who would.

"Oh, you betcha!" she said in a very strong Minnesota dialect. I was taken aback.

"Are you from Minnesota??"

"Yep. I came out here for a vacation 24 years ago, fell in love with the sunsets, and never went back," she proudly stated.

Considering the sunset I witnessed the previous night, I could understand her passion. However, even though I consider myself a rather spontaneous person, I don't think I could ever be that rash to just abandon my life for an eternal sunset. How I wish I could, though.

It reminded me of my great aunt and uncle, Helen and Dale, who one day in the mid-'60s finished lunch, went for a drive, and never came back. They ended up in California where they stayed for the rest of their lives. My mother told me she remembers their landlord calling for them since they left all their belongings in the apartment—they even left the dirty lunch dishes on the table. Now, I have always known that my family was full of the nomadic types. My great-grandparents had a homestead in western Nebraska in 1891, and some other relatives moved from Virginia to eastern Iowa as early as 1824 and were settled in western Iowa by the mid-1850s. I never thought of them being all that spontaneous without someone chasing them—which I like to think is why they traveled around so much back then. I mean really...who would move to western Iowa just a couple decades after Lewis and Clark buried Sgt. Floyd there? Only murderers and thieves, I reckon. Then again, times were hard and people went where opportunity was. Not to mention the thrill of the unknown is a definite draw. Desire for spontaneous adventure may be a genetic trait, it certainly explains a lot about me.

As I fired up Roxie, I realized I'd forgotten to ask the friendly Minnesota ex-pat for directions. The bright sunshine eliminated a lot of the variety of nature's colors from the night before, and the day promised to be hot. I loaded up the van and took a spin around town before getting back on the highway. I stopped at a feed store to take a gander at all the western wear in the hopes of finding either the elusive cowboy hat or sparkly turquoise ring. And lo and behold! There it was. A white straw cowboy hat with brown leather trim lit up brightly with the morning sun and called out to me from across the room! I rushed over to it, looked at the price tag, and it was less than $30! Hooray!! I slapped it on my head and; my goodness...I looked stunning.

I wore it around the store and didn't take it off all day. I picked up some snacks for the road, and even found some special dog treats (they were a dog and horse friendly establishment) for Judy who was sitting in the driver's seat in the van once again.

Highway 40 from Kingman to Albuquerque is a straight, long road. I had driven it several times before and remembered seeing Native American "Trading Posts" and the like scattered along it at rest stops. As I drove the highway this time, I noticed that the small, independently owned restaurants and stores were gone. Every exit on the highway now had a Subway restaurant and was serviced by Love's Travel Stops & Country Stores. All the souvenirs offered at these places were the same as the place before. They were the new version of the Stuckey's truck stops of my childhood in the Midwest. As the day droned on and on, I got less and less enthusiastic that I would see any remnants of the old Highway 66 culture at all.

U.S. Route 66, a.k.a. Will Rogers Highway, a.k.a. The Mother Road, a.k.a. Main Street of America was the main artery from Chicago to Los Angeles since 1926. It is quite possibly the most famous road in America.

Tom Joad and his family traveled the road in *The Grapes of Wrath*, Nat King Cole sang about it, and Lightning McQueen repaved part of it. It was the path of salvation for destitute sharecroppers during the depression, and the birthplace of McDonald's in 1940. It had a thriving tourist business that was in part driven by the kitschy attractions along the way, such as Wigwam Motels, the historic Round Barn, and the Gemini Giant.

In 1978 my family drove from southeastern Nebraska to Los Angeles for a vacation. Even though I was excited to go to Disneyland, I was never a big fan of these long drives my father insisted on taking us on every year. Part of the reason was that I was a kid and the destination was infinitely more important than the journey, and the other was that I would get carsick from reading in the backseat all day. To combat my inevitable upset stomach, my mother would give me Juicy Fruit gum (which didn't help at all) and warm 7-Up (which did.) And so, when my father made the decision to drive along Route 66 as much as he could, I wasn't happy because the detour was going to delay me meeting Mickey Mouse by a good half day. It meant I'd be queasy for that much longer. My whining didn't deter my dad because he knew something I didn't know. Route 66 was dying and he wanted to be sure his daughters saw it before it disappeared forever.

The Interstate Highway Act of 1956 marked the beginning of the end of Route 66, as newly constructed Interstate highways bypassed many of the small towns and tourist sites. The road and its towns fell into disrepair and ruin in the years since. Many parts of the original highway were broken up and removed. Roadside villages became ghost towns not unlike those left over from the Gold Rush. After decades of declining traffic, the road was finally decommissioned in 1985. In 1987 the first Route 66 association was founded in Arizona to help preserve the history of the road. As a result, some towns have revived to their heyday glory, and parts of Route 66 have become listed on the National Register of Historical Places. As wonderful as these improvements have been, today it is literally impossible to take Route 66 uninterrupted from Chicago to Los Angeles. That joy is gone forever.

As I now drove along highway 40, I thought back to that family trip along the Mother Road, and I suddenly wished I had been paying more attention back in '78. I remembered the small towns, the kitschy roadside attractions, and the Native American "Trading Posts" (I remember asking my dad if we had anything to trade with the Natives, and he laughed and replied, "Money,") but I didn't actually realize at the time that I would never see them again in the same way. It made me sad, and I spent the next couple of hours mourning the loss of what I feel is an important part of 20th Century Americana. Sad, that is, until I got to Meteor City!

Hooray! It was still there! Meteor City is one of six trading posts that used to line Route 66 across Arizona. It is the only one left. I excitedly screeched Roxie to a dusty halt in the parking lot and was inside the geodesic dome faster than you could say, "Jackalope."

It was perfect. There were literally thousands of Native American blankets, beadwork, baskets, and yes, turquoise jewelry. There was also Route 66 magnets, coffee mugs, key chains, etc. I hadn't seen this much kitschy fabulousness since the Trees of Mystery back in California. Needless to say, I spent quite a bit of time poring over the jewelry cases; however, I couldn't find anything that was what I wanted for an affordable price. I did find several gorgeous turquoise bracelets that I loved, but they cost several hundred dollars, and let's face it, I'm just too cheap to pay more for a bracelet than I did for my television. And so, back on the road I went, however, I was starting to feel like I was finally, finally in the Southwest.

My schedule for the day was to hit Albuquerque in time for dinner. Therefore, I didn't stop at the Petrified Forest, but I did check out the Painted Desert Indian Center. Once again, after viewing hundreds of turquoise items, I left despondent and empty-handed. Maybe it was road fatigue, but my patience for the ever-elusive turquoise ring was evaporating with the heat of the day. Miles and miles droned on as the temperature rose.

As dark started to fall, I was still quite a distance from that *magical, faraway place where the sun is always shining and the air smells like warm root beer and the towels are oh so fluffy*[1] ...and to make things even worse, I was stuck in the mother of Mother Road convoys. At least 100

---

1 *Lyrics from "Albuquerque" –"Weird Al" Yankovic, 1999*

semi trucks lined the road—all going in my direction. Two trucks led the pack, driving side-by-side, one in each lane, and kept all traffic at the same speed—slow. I was tired, cranky, and really not happy with this situation. Sure, I could have taken the next couple of hours pretending I was in a *Smokey and the Bandit* sequel, and we were merely hiding in the rocking chair eluding Buford T. Justice, but Judy definitely wasn't up for playing Fred to my Snowman. Basically, I whined and moaned and complained as my stomach growled in hunger and I irrationally bleated the horn periodically in frustration. What should have taken us less than an hour, took us two, and then we finally arrived in Albuquerque, New Mexico—the city where the *Shriners and the lepers play their ukuleles all day long and anyone on the street will gladly shave your back for a nickel.*[2]

2   *Lyrics from "Albuquerque" –"Weird Al" Yankovic, 1999*

Albuquerque, New Mexico, to Lubbock, Texas
Thursday, October 14, 2004

The alarm went off with a frightful screech. I bashed the snooze down as hard as I could and a feeling of pure terror came over me. Judy looked at me with joy in her eyes, and jumped on top of me to give me an early morning kiss, but I couldn't return the affection nor the enthusiasm for yet another day on the road. *I happen(ed) to wake up and find (my)self in an existential quandary full of loathing and self-doubt and wracked with the pain and isolation of (my) pitiful meaningless existence.*[3]

It all just seemed so hopeless that cold and frosty morning. I really, really wanted to be home. Steinbeck said that trips end when they end. Sometimes they end weeks after you get home, but that morning in Albuquerque, my trip ended. I was no longer excited about the journey. I was ready to get back into my regular life again. I wanted to sit in my living room and watch an old movie. I wanted to go out with my friends and laugh and eat and drink the night away, knowing that I'd fall asleep with my head on my own pillow, then wake up and go to my job at 8:30 a.m. I missed the routine of daily life. The constant motion of waking up, loading the van, reviewing *Travels with Charley*, driving for hours, filming what I needed to film, finding a motel, finding a restaurant, unloading the van, and sleeping fitfully in a strange bed knowing I'd only have to do it all again in the morning had lost its shimmer of newness. The shine started to dull in central California, and this morning it finally tarnished. I was done.

---

3 *Lyrics from "Albuquerque" –"Weird Al" Yankovic, 1999 (Last one, I promise. Who knew "Weird Al" was so prophetic?)*

Hmm...I thought. Why don't I just bag it all for now and go home? I could sell the van and catch a flight...and, no. No, I couldn't catch a flight. I had a van full of belongings I couldn't ship home. Heck, I had a dog I couldn't ship home. Maybe I could cut up to Colorado and bee-line home in a couple of days? No. No matter how I tried to drive home, I was at least a week away. If I had someone fresh to drive with me, we could drive straight through in about 36 hours, provided there were no mechanical, weather, or road construction issues. But alas, I ain't got nobody.

So there it was. In the stark light of that harsh New Mexico morning, I realized I was at least a week from home. I burst into tears.

After a very long and painful crying jag that also included some door slamming and Kleenex throwing, I finally flopped down on the bed, emotionally spent. Judy immediately hopped on the bed and lay down next to me. She timidly smooshed her nose into my face and licked my nose. Then she burrowed her face into my neck. I felt my sanity slowly resume. After all, I wasn't truly alone. Judy was with me. I hugged her tight and after a couple of minutes, she sneezed, tried to lick my face but missed, then sneezed again, and flipped over belly-up so I could rub her tummy, her tail pounding on the bed like a metronome. And just like that, she brought me back from the depths of despair into which I had sunk. I was still desirous of being home, but at least I no longer felt beaten. After all, the best way out of an unpleasant situation is through it. And so, I dried my tears, took a deep breath and vowed to soldier onward. (After all, what other choice did I have?) I loaded up the van one more time. I shifted my focus to the thought that perhaps today I would finally find that elusive turquoise ring I so desired. Considering my bad track record on that front, I wasn't too optimistic, but I decided to see what Albuquerque's Old Town had to offer. At the very least, a little sightseeing might lift my spirits.

I bumbled out into the frigid and rainy weather that was as depressing as my mood. Even Judy seemed more subdued than usual as she hopped into the van and settled in the back. We drove around town and I was reminded once again at how welcoming and lovely Albuquerque is.

On my family's Route 66 trip back in 1978, we also stayed a night in Albuquerque. The next morning, we woke up to lovely sunshine and surrounded by flowering roads, clean surroundings, and fresh air. We were so moved by the scenery we decided to delay our departure a while and drove around town, gawking at the sparkling oasis of color and greenery in the middle of the dusty desert. We all agreed we could see ourselves living happily in this emerald city, that is, until my father mentioned, "You know, the only problem would be that there isn't anything around here for 100 miles." Considering we lived in Beatrice, Nebraska, that seemed like an odd comment, but Beatrice was only 40 miles from Lincoln, and you can drive 40 miles for dinner. Even with this sort of long-distance perspective, 100 miles is a full-day round-trip journey at the bare minimum. And so, even though this beautiful New Mexico city no doubt had everything we could possibly need or desire, we all agreed we would feel too isolated to live there on a permanent basis. And so, with the taste of sour grapes lingering in our mouths, we headed back on the road.

Old Town Albuquerque is completely different from the rest of the cosmopolitan downtown. Wandering down the brick streets lined with adobe buildings all painted in hues of yellows and rust, I suddenly imagined myself in a cotton skirt and ruffled blouse, gold hoop earrings dangling in my ears. The sound of soft guitar music swells from a neighboring window, and a donkey cart rumbles around the corner, covered with colorful fruits and vegetables for sale. My espadrilles skip along the path, until I find the wrought-iron doorway to my casa. Inside, I can smell the tapas my mother is cooking in the kitchen. I feel myself blush as I realize she wouldn't approve of my plans to meet Pablo behind the mission at dusk. Oh, Pablo. His piercing eyes and strong shoulders were burned in my soul. But his family was wealthy and his grandfather had murdered my grandfather in a duel over land rights...eh. Something tells me I've read too many Barbara Cartland novels. Ahem. Meanwhile, back to reality...

Old Town Albuquerque is cute. Very, very cute. There are lots of jewelry stores and boutiques, and after entering exactly two, I found myself in turquoise ring heaven. Tanner Chaney jewelers had my ring for sale. It was oval with a greenish turquoise stone and was designed by a local Native Artist. As they processed my transaction, I was told that the stone had come from Pilot Mountain mine in Nevada.

"How do you know that?" I asked.

"You can tell from the color and marbleizing of the stone," my friendly and informative sales rep replied.

I was impressed. I also found out a great deal about turquoise.

For instance, I didn't know there are only two turquoise mines in New Mexico. Most veins are located in Arizona, Nevada, and Utah. Surprisingly enough, although I definitely associate turquoise with the American Southwest, the ancient Egyptians and Persians have been utilizing turquoise for thousands of years. It is considered a holy stone and was worn as a talisman for good luck. Even the iconic burial mask of King Tutankhamun is inlaid with turquoise. Considering I have always had an intensive interest in ancient Egypt, due to a book I read on mummification when I was 14, I considered this to be just one more validation to spend the money on this gorgeous piece of jewelry. As I pulled out my credit card, the sun burst through the gray cloud cover and all was right with the world.

As I headed out of town into the midday sun, I looked back in my rearview mirror and sadly watched Albuquerque disappear behind me. What a beautiful city.

After driving for what seemed like (and was) hours, I was starting to get road weary again. After all, one can only handle so much beautiful Southwestern nature at a time, and I was starting to suffer from gorgeous overload. Also, Judy needed to go potty.

With Texas on the horizon, I noticed a sign for Glenrio. I decided to take a break and see what was left of this famous Route 66 ghost town.

Glenrio, Texas/New Mexico, is one of the many small towns that were bustling stops on the Mother Road that no doubt Steinbeck drove through. However, once the Interstate bypassed it, these small towns ceased to be. In 2004, there's nothing much left except for a few decaying buildings, frozen in time. The post office. A gas station. A motel. Everything worth anything was taken from there long ago; long before nature started taking back its claim on the land. Bushes and tumbleweeds were growing up in parking lots, and signs were battered and broken from decades of wind. Vermin and snakes now temporarily resided in the motel, and the only sign of human life was...wait. There wasn't any. Route 66 itself was cracked and crumbling. I may have been the only person to drive on that stretch of road in a week or more. And yet, about a half mile away, I could see the trucks and cars zipping along highway 40, not knowing that Glenrio existed. It was truly heartbreaking.

After Judy relieved herself near the signpost that declared "The First Motel in Texas" on one side, and "The Last Motel in Texas" on the other, we climbed back into Roxie and fought back the urge to cry at the loss of a life we never knew.

Texas! Mighty, mighty Texas. It laid bare before us ripe with opportunity and adventure. The Alamo! The Dallas Cowboys! Buddy Holly's birthplace! And, uh...lots of other stuff I didn't know about yet. And once we left the Lone Star State, I would finally be in Louisiana—a state I'd never seen. But first we had three days of TexMex, "Howdy ya'll!"s, and oil wells ahead of us.

The plan was to drive through Amarillo and arrive in Lubbock in time for dinner. I have to admit every time I see the word "Amarillo," I think "armadillo." I know that's incorrect, but I think the town should adopt a photo of an armadillo as their town logo because it would totally justify my thought process.

The landscape turned dusty. I was expecting to see lots of cattle and oil wells along the way, but so far all I'd seen was low trees and cacti. Tumbleweeds grew everywhere. It felt lonely, yet not desolate. I was expecting a little more jovial area, most likely because I had just passed a town named "Happy." Maybe it was, but the surrounding area was lonelier. Then again, maybe I was just feeling the lonely ache of the road? It's hard to say.

Scooting along the country roads, I found myself relaxing and taking in the scenery. I have to admit while zipping along the Interstate for the past couple hundred miles, relaxing was something I had gotten out of the habit of doing. On the Interstate, it's all about covering distance. But here, in the middle of Texas, I found myself slowing down, leaning back in my seat, and gawking at the rolling hills and barren fields. Occasionally, I'd round a bend and there, perched in a neighboring field, was a lovely new house. A winding drive led up to the large parking area in front of the two-story, brown-sided building, and just beyond the corner of the garage I cold see a colorful new jungle gym with a slide and swing. Beyond the jungle gym, there was nothing but scenery—rolling hills, cacti and bushes of all colors, layers of white and gray clouds dotting the rapidly reddening sky, and then miles away, the horizon. How stunning. How beautiful. Just like that, I was back on vacation.

Since I meandered along through the lovely countryside, I was late getting into Lubbock. I stopped at the first motel I could find (they had WiFi, but I didn't have any wireless capabilities, so it was lost on me), and asked the clerk at the desk if she could recommend a place to eat.

She lit up and practically yelled, "The Copper Caboose!"

I was a bit taken aback by her enthusiasm, so I asked what was so special about that place?

"It's a blast! You'll love it," was the only reply I got. So, OK then. The Copper Caboose it was.

After unloading the van and feeding/watering Judy, we headed about a half mile down the road to the very conveniently located Copper Caboose. It was easy to find, since it was a long, low building at the back of a massive parking lot that was completely full of cars, trucks, SUVs, and motorcycles. Boy, I thought, this must be a good place.

I parked the van in a shady spot in the parking lot, which I suspect was further away from the front door than my hotel was, and started the long journey toward food. Twenty minutes later, it seemed, I was still walking. The sun was starting to set, and I strongly suspected I made a wrong turn back at a red Chevy one-ton pickup with jacked-up, oversized wheels, and yellow pin-striping on the tailgate, when suddenly, as I stepped out of the shadow of a black Hummer with tinted windows and silver wheels, there it was in all its glory...THE COPPER CABOOSE. I was amazed at the popularity of such a non-descript institution. It looked like a very large VFW. When I stepped inside the door, it became immediately clear why the place was so popular. It was a poker joint.

In 2004, televised poker was in its infancy, and I'd yet to see it. Yet, here in Lubbock, it seemed to be the community's favorite pastime. Miles upon miles of poker tables were spread throughout the massive room to my right, while families chowed down in the restaurant on my left. I turned left, got a lovely seat in a booth and ordered a small beer. When the waiter returned, he sat a goldfish bowl on a pedestal down in front of me. It was bigger than my head, and full of beer.

"Wait!" I yelled after him. "I think you made a mistake. I ordered a small beer."

"That is a small, ma'am," he replied. "It's the only size we have."

I. Love. Texas.

After a very filling and fulfilling dinner of chicken quesadillas and a small beer, I was fat and sleepy beyond belief. Judy was snoozing in the van all the way back to the motel. I, too, was quite happy in Texas. In my pocket was a receipt for that gallon of beer. It cost $2.75.

Lubbock, Texas, to Austin, Texas
Friday, October 15, 2004

John Steinbeck spent a large portion of the time in Texas at a family friend's home. He rattled on in detail about the wealth of said friends, and then went fishing and cooked and ate his catch himself. He was wistful remembering the simple joys that large sums of money can buy.

As much as I would have liked to have sought out said ranch and laze about for a few days, I was not allowed such luxury. I had a schedule to keep. I did, however, take a bit of a detour at one point because I noticed there was a small town off the main road named Baird. My mother's maiden name is Baird, and we have a photo of my aunt and uncle standing next to the town sign from one of their many vacations years ago. I thought it would be great to get a photo of myself in front of it to send to them.

I pulled into Baird, and it looked just like a million other small towns and I was thrilled to see a Dairy Queen! I pulled over, purchased a Dilly Bar for myself, a puppy cone for Judy, and we sat under the shade of a tree and enjoyed the creamy, icy goodness that took me back to my childhood. Dairy Queen played such an important role in my growing up. It was a reward for good grades, a consolation prize when my t-ball team lost the big game, and the place to sit and watch the 4th of July parade. We were fortunate enough to have two Dairy Queens in Beatrice, so there was one conveniently located on the way home from Riverside Park's swimming pool, and another on the way to the Safeway store. When I got older, the DQ (as it was by then called) was a hangout where we'd meet up with other kids we'd see cruising the main loop down 6th Street, turn left at Court Street, drive-through the Arctic Circle parking lot (after checking to see who had brought out their motorcycles on the off-chance we could bum a ride once around the loop), head back on Court Street, turn right up 6th Street, circle through McDonald's parking lot (after being checked out by the people inside on the off-chance they could bum a ride once around the loop), then make a left on 6th again and start all over again. Sometimes you'd see someone you wanted to talk to, so you'd flash your lights and yell, "Pull over at the DQ!" They'd flash their recognition, and then you'd meet up with them a few minutes later. It sounds boring to describe it, but in fact, it was a lot of fun. And back in the late 1970s in Beatrice, Nebraska, cruising is what teens did for social activity after watching *The Dukes of Hazzard*. Funny how something as small as a Dilly Bar can transport you across the years and miles...

Speaking of miles, Texas is so big...(How big is it?) It is so big, it takes three days to drive across. It's larger than France and Austria combined. Even knowing this fact, it's still hard to get a clear perception on exactly how big it truly is until you are sitting behind the wheel for 1,115 hours. Even for a person who grew up in one of those big states located west of the Mississippi, it still never seems to end. Yes, I know Alaska is technically larger than Texas, but the bulk of Alaska isn't inhabited—at least not on the scale of Texas. As I blew along the dusty road, field upon field stretched from the ditch to the horizon. Telephone wires were the only things blocking the view. As far as I could see, I was probably viewing only one farm. Everything in Texas just seems bigger. For instance...God.

So far throughout the trip, I'd seen many religious billboards. It's always been a part of America and it always will be. Back in Vermont, I saw signs of churches listing their bingo nights. In North Dakota, I saw signs discouraging abortion with threat of damnation. But Texas is the only place I actually saw one from the Almighty himself.

"Stop by my house Sunday before the game! –God" one sign said. It was a great selling point. I bet he has the best Buffalo wings at his Super Bowl party.

With my limited Congregational faith I have to admit I was starting to feel a tad unworthy of such fire and brimstone blasting at me from signs in the middle of nowhere. Were there more Christians in Texas than anywhere else, or were the people in Texas just more vocal about their faith? I pulled over at a Trucker's Chapel that was a trailer behind the diesel pumps at a rest stop on my quest for answers.

The chapel was closed.

I was initially disappointed, but then I remembered that the Lord moves in mysterious ways. Perhaps the answers I was seeking weren't available to me in a roadside chapel? Perhaps I needed to only look into myself for the deeper meanings of life? Perhaps next time I go searching for my heart's desire I won't look any further than my own back yard? I think the meaning of life can be best summed up in a Ziggy cartoon I've had on my refrigerator for about 20 years. Ziggy has finally reached an old guru on a mountain, and looks up at him eager to hear nuggets of life wisdom from the guru's ancient, cracked lips. The guru speaks, "Life? Life is just one darn thing after another. I thought everyone knew that."

With my quest for religion temporarily thwarted, I took Judy for a hop and a skip around the rest area. Judy, Judy, Judy. The girl never ceases to amaze me. She has never had any such spiritual quandaries, I am sure. Her capacity for love is limitless. She has no ego or shame to restrict her ability to express her love to anyone at anytime. Her ability to be enraptured by the minutest tuft of grass for minutes on end speaks of a greater appreciation for life than I will ever know. Her committed passion to the eradication of all other dogs is an irrefutable fact, yet she offers no apologies. Oh, but if only I could be so comfortable with my own virtues and vices, there would be no need for spiritual exploration or enlightenment. If only humans were able to be as accepting of life as dogs are. As Steinbeck said about Charley, "certainly his horizons were limited, but how broad are mine?" I prefer to sum it up thusly...Dog spelled backwards is God. Amen.

This day was the day that road fatigue finally set in with a vengeance. I felt the rhythm of the road humming along underneath me for mile after mile of scrubby landscape that was periodically punctuated by cacti and tumbleweeds. Fences lined the gargantuan fields. The sun beat down on Roxie's metal roof, and Judy found relief from the heat by sitting in the passenger seat and sticking her face into the cold wind blasting from the air conditioner. As I sat cozily cool in my comfortable seat, I set the cruise control to 60, leaned back, and relaxed my left foot up on the dash. The drive may have been long, but it was comfortable. I somewhat guiltily was relieved to be traveling in such creature comforts rather than the old RV. There is truly something wonderful about the finer things.

My arrival in Austin was unremarkable. It was dark and I was tired. All I wanted to do was to get to a motel, grab dinner, and hit the hay. The clerk at the motel recommended a steakhouse just down the road, which sounded like the perfect relaxing ending to the long day.

Two hours later...

I finally got seated at the steakhouse. Considering how many steakhouses there must be in Austin, you know, Texas, I was shocked at how crowded and popular this particular one was. Everyone there seemed to be jovial and happy and having a lovely time chewing their steak and all, and it appeared I was the only one looking for a quick meal and bed. I was incredibly cranky by the time I sat down. Lucky for me, my waiter was quick and efficient and within a half hour I had ordered, eaten, and was out the door. I think that's one of the few times in my life that my wait to get a table was longer than the actual meal. Was it worth it? I can't remember. In fact, I don't even remember the name of the restaurant. I can only say that at least I didn't hate it, so in hindsight, it must have been spectacular food to offset the frustration of the wait for a table.

Austin, Texas, to Baton Rouge, Louisiana
Saturday, October 16, 2004

After the great luck I had finding my hat and ring, since I hit Texas, I had been searching for yet another fine souvenir of this journey. I wanted something else that represented America. Something considered the world over as an image synonymous with this great country. Something people in Europe shun. Something I couldn't even find in New England. I wanted a symbol of the hearty men and women who kissed their families goodbye, left their homelands forever, and strode bravely into the harsh, unknown New World, hoping to find the land of milk and honey, and if not, well, whatever lay ahead would hopefully be better than what they were leaving behind. An emblem of all the good things about this great country of mine...you know...a big-a** Western-style belt buckle.

Yes, I was on the search for a sparkly, silvery belt buckle just like the ones my pilgrim ancestors wore when they hopped off *The Mayflower*. My Irish kinfolk arrived significantly later than the English blokes—somewhere around 1730—and I picture them wearing white fisherman's sweaters and knickers. However, no doubt both sides of the family proudly displayed their buckles on their shoes rather than their belts, of course, but the American buckle-wearing tradition carries on even to this day. I wanted one that proudly proclaimed, "AMERICA. LOVE IT OR LEAVE IT" and weighed more than Judy. Or perhaps one with a bas relief image of a bucking bronco—or maybe one with just a red, white, and blue flag surrounded with rhinestones. As long as it was a hunk of metal that was large enough to double as a dinner plate, I would be happy. And I knew that if I couldn't find such a thing in Texas, then I couldn't find it anywhere.

I awoke on my second day in the Lone Star State still on my quest. I had found plenty of leather goods, hats, even alligator souvenirs, but not one single belt buckle had so far appeared along my path. I was again surprised at the homogenization of the roadside stops from earlier in my childhood. I remember every gas station from the Mississippi to the Pacific Ocean carrying souvenir belt buckles. A lot of the time they were even lined up next to the cash register as if they were impulse buys. However, in 2004, it seems they have gone out of style—at least with the tourist stops.

In *Travels with Charley*, Steinbeck didn't really have much to say about this great state. Considering it took him at least as long as it took me to cross it, I would have thought he'd have been more chatty about it, but he wasn't. I understand his familial gathering in Texas seems to have been the focus of his time there, so maybe it isn't that odd after all, but all I know is, the next major place he discusses in detail is New Orleans.

But first I had to mess with Texas. Have I mentioned it's a big state? After fighting my way through road construction on the fringes of Austin and flying like an eagle to the sea, I finally found myself zipping past the shining skyline of Houston—still buckle-less and losing hope.

Just before the Louisiana border, I caught sight of a sign offering western wear. After making a double take, I slammed on the brakes and took the exit to The Horseman's Store. Smoke poured from my tires as I threw gravel in the parking lot. Judy woke up and leapt into the passenger seat, and sneezed a couple of time. Whoops...sorry, old girl.

I couldn't believe my luck! I hopped quickly out of Roxie, and practically ran to the door of the shop. I pulled open the big wooden door, and stepped into the cool air that smelled of leather and tanning products. I knew—I just knew I was going to find a belt buckle here.

There were boots, and hats, and buckles, and belts, and friendly staff eager to sell any and all of the products to me! Since I was on a tight schedule, I knew I had to divide and conquer, so I instantly narrowed the buckle options down to two. One was a silver relief of an outdoor scene with a howling wolf. There was turquoise inlay and it was very beautiful. It was very Native American in style. The other was a silver belt buckle with a Texas Longhorn steer's head smack dab in the center. I discussed the options with the salesclerk, and within seconds realized I already had my turquoise ring representing the Southwest. I needed a Texas souvenir, so the Longhorn won out. Ten minutes later, I was walking—nay, swaggering—out the door with my dusty Levi's held in place with a wide black hand-tooled leather belt and The Mighty Bevo shining proudly just below my belly button.

Before I got back in the van, I looked across the expansive vista, taking it all in one more time. Then, as I climbed aboard and fired up Roxie for the last time in Texas, I found myself humming a song I hadn't heard in quite a while:

Don't bury me in this prairie
Take me where the cement grows
Let's move down to some big town
Where they love a gal by the cut o' her clothes
And I'll stand out
In buttons and bows...[4]

By golly, I felt snazzy.

The day grew longer, and the heat grew wetter. I finally found myself in Louisiana for the first time in my life. It was surreal. The highway unfurled through swamplands of the likes I'd never seen. Bridge after bridge spanned bayous that were littered with trees, infested with bugs, and most likely home to a few alligators. I hate alligators.

---

4 *"Buttons and Bows" Music by Jay Livingston. Lyric by Ray Evans. 1947*

Focusing on the road ahead, and trying not to imagine what would happen if, say, the road collapsed while I was driving over one of those tsetse fly-riddled bogs, I gunned for Baton Rouge.

Baton Rouge is the capitol of Louisiana. I only knew this because of the *Brady Bunch* episode when Cindy won the chance to compete on *Question the Kids* with Monty Hall, and she froze up when asked, "What is the capitol of Louisiana?" Watching the live show from home, Marcia says to the petrified Cindy on TV, "Come on, Cindy. You know this! Baton Rouge! Baton Rouge!"

Who says TV isn't educational?

The only other things I knew for certain about Baton Rouge is that the state capitol building is the tallest in the country, and that it reminds me a lot of the state capitol building in Nebraska.

As a kid in Beatrice, my family used to drive the 40 miles into Lincoln pretty much every weekend. Since Nebraska is very flat, and the capitol was by far the tallest building in the city, it was the first part of the skyline that would come into view as we approached town. In order to keep my sister and me occupied during the 45-minute ride, my parents created the "Who can see the capitol building first?" challenge. Usually, my sister won, merely because she was older, and therefore, taller, so she had a slight sight-line advantage. Then again, this was before the days of seat belts, and I remember standing on the backseat and leaning over the middle of the front seat between my parents to try to get a better view. Funny. Nowadays, my parents would probably be held for questioning by children services for child endangerment, but back then, I needed the extra angle to actually be competitive. Spotting the capitol building was a fun game for quite a while until my dad pointed out that it is visible from the first small hill outside of Princeton, Nebraska, an amazingly 18 miles away. Once we knew that, well, it really wasn't much of a challenge anymore, so we switched to license plate bingo.

I really shouldn't have been surprised at the similarity between the Nebraska capitol building and the Louisiana capitol building since the Nebraska one was the inspiration for the Louisiana one. The Baton Rouge architects even added sculptures by Lee Lawrie, who sculpted the iconic "The Sower" on the top of the Lincoln capitol. Sure, they had to one-up Nebraska's by building it 15 stories higher, but Lincoln's is still the *heaviest* capitol building in the country, so there. (Go Huskers!)

The biggest surprise about Baton Rouge was the heat. This wasn't the dusty, windblown, dry heat of Texas and the Southwest. This was a wet, muggy, sodden, smothering, sweaty, sluggish heat. Stepping out of Roxie's placid and refreshing air-conditioning, I felt the sopping wet blanket of oppressive heat wrap tightly around me, and left my lungs gasping for air that wasn't soaked with moisture. It was horrible. I complained loudly to the motel desk clerk and asked if it was always this hot. "I guess it is a little humid," she replied.

A little? Stepping back out into the stagnant, stifling heat, I was instantly drenched in sweat—sweat that wouldn't dry out until I got safely into the luxurious dry air-conditioning of the motel. To make sure I wasn't just having premature hot flashes, once I got into the room, I checked the Weather Channel. Sure enough, I was right. It was officially 10,000 degrees with two million percent humidity. Ha!

Judy, too, wasn't too happy with the weather. After getting in the room, she lethargically drank some water, jumped onto the bed, circled around three times, then lay down facing the airconditioner, and closed her eyes with a heavy sigh. That's where we stayed for the rest of the night.

Baton Rouge, Louisiana, to Montgomery, Alabama
Sunday, October 17, 2004

The Big Easy, my eye. New Orleans was a town of secrets and scandal. Crime and punishment. Death and rebirth. Jelly Roll Morton and Anne Rice. There ain't nothin' easy about it, and I couldn't wait to get there. I'd never been there, but I could see my arrival there as clear as day...

Fade in on a street in the French Quarter.

Sunrise.

An old Creole woman is riding down the street with a wagon pulled by a small mule singing about her wares. A young man with dark hair is sitting quietly on a balcony watching her. The rest of the town is still asleep when he sings down to her, softly at first, but gaining strength as his rich baritone resonates between the buildings.

"Crawfish, craaawfish."

"Craaawfish," the woman replies.

Elvis continues singing while sending her smoldering looks, finishes the song, has a fight with his father, gets kicked out of school, runs into trouble, meets a girl, saves Morticia Addams from Walter Mattheau, sings some more, fights the bad guy, loses the girl, is unable to save Morticia Addams from the bad guy (at her awesome dockside home), gets the girl and sings again while the credits roll and his father watches with pride.

Therefore, when I arrived in town, I was surprised to see a very large, very modern city. It reminded me of Chicago for some reason. I wasn't actually disappointed, but I was less than excited. I pulled over to search the map to try to locate the two places of interest from *Travels with Charley*—the first was a cemetery with a quizzical epitaph of one Robert John Cresswell, died 1845 aged 26, that Steinbeck mentioned:

Alas that one whose darnthly joy had often to trust in heaven should canty thus sudden to from all its hopes benivens and though thy love for off remore that dealt the dog pest thou left to prove they sufferings while below.

He said he almost knew what it meant. I hadn't the faintest. However, I wanted to find the tombstone in the St. Louis cemetery. Imagine my surprise to find that there isn't just one St. Louis cemetery, nor is there two. There are three, count 'em, three—and Mr. Steinbeck wasn't kind enough to let me know which one housed his favorite epitaph. Since I was not in the mood to search more than one burial ground for said landmark—after all, there was jazz to hear, hurricanes to drink, and Elvis to meet down in the French Quarter—I decided Steinbeck was referring to St. Louis Cemetery #1 because it was just around the corner from where I'd parked. Judy and I set off on the short walk, crossed a street, and followed the white wall of the cemetery around to the front entrance gate.

It was closed.

Is nothing in this country open on a Sunday afternoon?

I took some photographs of the cemetery through the gate, and dejectedly shuffled off to try to locate my second *Travels with Charley*-themed destination—the William Franz Elementary School.

In 1954, the U.S. Supreme Court passed a landmark decision in *Brown vs. the Board of Education* declaring that public schools must be integrated. As with all things government, it took several years for the ruling to be implemented, and in the fall of 1960, the first school was finally integrated. The city was New Orleans, the school was the William Franz

Elementary School, and the first black student to enter a white school was a little six-year-old girl named Ruby Bridges.

Steinbeck spoke at length about the news coverage and the protests by "The Cheerleaders" that were in process upon his arrival in New Orleans. He made a point of seeing the protests in person, and he left feeling anxious about what the future would bring to the country. Civil Rights was still in its infancy then, and the fear of a race war was as palpable as the fear of a nuclear one.

When I was a little girl, I saw a print of Norman Rockwell's, *The Problem We All Live With*, which is a painting of the scene in New Orleans that Steinbeck witnessed firsthand. In fact, legend has it that Steinbeck's description of the event is what inspired Rockwell to paint his famous portrait of the little girl wearing a starched white dress, socks, and shoes walking stoically to the left of the frame, while large, headless men with "Deputy U.S. Marshall" armbands on their sleeves surround her in a protective square. On the wall she is calmly passing, written just over her beribboned pigtails, is the word, "N**GER" and the remnants of a hurled tomato is splattered at the end as a bloody punctuation mark. That painting terrified me. I was so frightened for that girl, and I knew that if I was her (and I was about her age when I first saw it), I would have been scared to death and crying for my mother. Instead, there was this little girl bravely striding forward towards school without any fear. In Steinbeck's story he said she even took a little hop at one point, and he surmised the reason was because she may have never gone more than ten steps in her life without skipping. This innocent, little girl was the focal point of some of the most transparent hatred anyone may ever have to witness, and yet she faced her enemies with bravery seldom seem. Because this little girl had parents who believed in equality, decided their daughter deserved a better world, and raised her to be brave and not afraid—this little girl stepped out of a car, walked into a school, and changed history forever. It awed me.

I stopped at a gas station not far from the St. Louis cemetery, and asked the clerk where I could find the school that Ruby Bridges integrated, and the lady said, "Oh! That school. Yeah…it's around here somewhere…Leticia? Where's that school that that little girl integrated??" I was flabbergasted. For a local citizen to not know where this historical site was completely baffled me. It seemed like the equivalent of a Minneapolis resident not knowing where Mary Tyler Moore threw her hat (note: In front of the old Donaldson's store at 7th and Nicollet Mall). However, Leticia knew, and she gave me specific and correct directions.

As I drove over to the school, I tried to imagine what life was like back in the days of segregation. For someone of my generation or younger, it's almost impossible to imagine, and yet it was a way of life from the beginnings of this country until the mid-20th century. Civil Rights was not a new idea in 1960. In fact, the Civil Rights Act of 1875 states:

Be it enacted, That all persons within the jurisdiction of the United States shall be entitled to the full and equal enjoyment of the accommodations, advantages, facilities, and privileges of inns, public conveyances on land or water, theaters, and other places of public amusement; subject only to the conditions and limitations established by law, and applicable alike to citizens of every race and color, regardless of any previous condition of servitude.

In other words, people could not be denied public service based on race. This was passed by Congress and signed into law a mere ten years after the end of the Civil War. However, it was seldom enforced, and by 1883, it was declared unconstitutional. "Separate but equal" Jim Crow laws were to remain in effect for the next 80 years.

By 1960 the Civil Rights movement had been slowly building steam. Even before Rosa Parks sparked the Montgomery Bus Boycott of 1955 because she refused to give up her seat on the bus to a white person, there were dozens of cases brought to trial and dozens of milestones reached in the slow movement toward equality.

I have thought about how to write about this few-mile journey to the segregated past, and I've found it difficult to explain. Mainly, I feel I can best express it by merely stating the tagline from Ruby Bridges' Foundation, "Racism is a grown up disease. Let's stop using kids to spread it." The fact that there is a need for Ruby's foundation in the 21st Century is a sad testament to how slowly socialized fears evolve.

It totally baffles me how in this day and age that racism could even still be an issue, but Ruby Bridges is correct. Children are not born to hate or fear someone based on their skin color. Racism is taught. Even today, with the first African-American President in the White House, people are still teaching their children to hate, and it's truly shameful. Will the disease ever be cured? I hope so. We can't rewrite history, but we can write a better future.

All these thoughts were swirling in my brain as I drove across town to the school where it all started. Poverty surrounded me. Graffiti-marked boarded-up houses lined the streets and I wondered if this area was this poor in 1960. Who lived in these little bungalows back then? Could this area have been home to middle-class, suburban folks back then? It was very easy to imagine. Little corner grocery stores, mechanics, insurance offices, and the like, could very well have dotted this neighborhood with well-maintained houses with neatly kept lawns. But in 2004 everything was dirty, dilapidated, or abandoned. I saw no people.

After a few blocks, the neighborhood started looking a bit more spiffed-up. The houses looked lived in. I started seeing people outside their homes. I turned a corner, and there it was, so much larger than I imagined it would be, The William Franz Public School.

I suddenly felt like a voyeur. This building was an active school that was well maintained and clean. There was nothing out of the ordinary about the place, and it was tremendously quiet. I didn't know what I expected to find there, but it was hard to imagine this peaceful school being surrounded by hostile, angry, white people hurling profane racial comments past the police and in the direction of a small child who was just walking into school. It boggles the mind to imagine. And yet it did happen, and it happened here.

Even though it was a Sunday, I decided to see if the school might, perhaps, be unlocked. I parked Roxie across the street in the shade, and hopped out. I felt foolish and a bit embarrassed. It was almost like I was a sinner and treading on sacred ground where I had no right to go. And then I saw something that made me very sad. There was a sign on the building that said, "No weapons allowed on school property" with a picture of a handgun with a circle around it and a line through it. This was an elementary school. It appears the conflict at this institution has never ceased; it's only changed forms. The holy reverence I was feeling was only my projections. In fact, the school was largely and unofficially segregated once again, only this time, the school is mainly black students. The neighborhood, too, had changed and the once middle-class community had suffered a downfall in the past 44 years. As the sign on the building revealed, crime was now no stranger to the area.

And yet, while I stood on that famous sidewalk, a small boy rode down the street on his bicycle. Lawn mowers hummed in the distance. Birds chirped on the telephone wires. I felt no fear. I felt pride. Those horrible walks that a little girl endured in 1960 resulted in the ultimate downfall of accepted racism in this country. And she did it peacefully, gracefully and without fear.

Before I took this trip, I managed to catch one of Ruby Bridges' lectures at the Clifford G. Beers Guidance Clinic's Builders breakfast in New Haven, Connecticut. I was hoping to meet her and talk to her about my project in the hopes that she might be interested in granting me an interview for this book. Before she spoke, I found my way over to her table and introduced myself. She expressed interest and said she needed to know more about it before she could make a decision. In subsequent weeks and months, I did follow up with her, but alas, the timing was never possible. It's too bad because she is a phenomenal speaker and for me to try to tell her story on her behalf is, well, like trying to paraphrase Steinbeck. It would only be a mediocre facsimile of greatness. All I can say is, if you ever are fortunate enough to get the chance to hear Ruby speak, do yourself a favor and go. The woman is as remarkable as the child.

Much as Steinbeck left New Orleans with more questions about the future of race relations in America, and so did I. Heading out of town, I actually found myself relieved. I was heading home. *Travels with Charley* ends shortly after Steinbeck leaves New Orleans. I guess he was just tired of traveling. To wit:

"My own journey started long before I left, and was over before I returned. I know exactly where and when it was over. Near Abingdon, in the dog-leg of Virginia, at four o'clock of a windy afternoon, without warning or good-by or kiss my foot, my journey went away and left me stranded far from home."

Like Steinbeck, my journey also ended before I got home. It really ended that horrible morning in Albuquerque a few days earlier. But now that officially, the bulk of my journey was over, I felt relieved, relaxed, and pointed Roxie's nose towards home.

I drove quickly through the rest of the day, and took a brief detour from Steinbeck's route to pick off the corner of Florida. There were two reasons for this change of plans. One was that I'd never been in Florida before. The other was because I just wanted to see what damage still remained a month after Hurricane Ivan.

The road along the Gulf of Mexico was open to traffic, but devastation littered the shoulders and ditches for miles on end. Trees were ripped up from their roots. Roofs had been blown off buildings. Land-moving equipment sat parked next to debris from lord knows where. It would no doubt be many months more before this area of the country looked normal again. I can't imagine what it must have been like to have experienced the storm at its worst. By the time Hurricane Ivan reached my home a thousand miles north, it had weakened to a low-pressure disturbance. However, on September 16 when it hit Alabama, it was a full force, category 3 hurricane, with winds around 120 mph, and was the size of Texas. I have never been in such a ferocious act of nature, and I hope never to be.

The closest I can possibly imagine is that a hurricane is like the biggest, baddest, longest, most violent tornado storm ever. I've had more than my share of exposure to tornados. After all, they are a weekly occurrence in southeastern Nebraska during the summertime, so my friends and I grew up trained in what to do when the tornado sirens would sound. The first thing you do is look at the sky. Considering you can see a good 30 miles in pretty much every direction, you can tell which direction the tornado is approaching from. The second thing you do is turn on a radio to hear where exactly it's located. Much like the blackjack player has the set rule of drawing on 16 and sticking on 17, the rule of thumb for tornados was, if it was spotted less than a mile from where you are, go to the basement. If you are in a car, get out of it. The absolute last place you want to be in a tornado is in a car. Whatever you do, do not try to outrun the tornado (it will win) or get closer to get a good video of it (it doesn't like being photographed). Get your butt out of the car as quickly as you can and lay facedown in a ditch by the road and cover your head. Do not take solace under trees or any structure that could fall on you/twist around you/ impale you through it like a toothpick through a pickle. Blades of straw have been forced through trees. Cars have ended up on top of houses. This is not a force to trifle with.

The good news is—the devastation is over within minutes! Seconds, sometimes. So, when the siren sounds, and the tornado is spotted less than a mile away, you hit the dirt for about five minutes, maximum. If it's more than a mile away, you keep playing softball because it's never going to sustain its power or path long enough to get to you. (Unless, of course, panic hits you, in which case you hit the dirt anyway, but if your friends aren't panicking, you feel rather silly.)

I remember vividly the closest I ever got to a tornado. I was 16 years old and over at my friend Chris's house. We were watching TV with her parents in their basement when the weather alert interrupted our program. The tornado was less than a mile away, just past my home. The phone rang, and it was my mother telling me to get home. I had no intention of heading out of a safe basement and drive toward a tornado that was bearing down on me, but my mother demanded I, "Get home NOW! I want you home!" And so, Chris and her parents bewilderedly said goodbye and glanced nervously at the sky over my house as I got into my 1974 orange VW bug to drive home.

It was raining cats and dogs. The streets were deserted as I gunned the little car as fast as it would go. My eyes were focused not on the road, but on the black and gray and white clouds directly in front of me. Slowly, I saw the rotation pick up and the clouds form a circle and start reaching from the heavens toward my house.

"I'm going to die," I thought. "I hope I do. That'll teach Mom," my arrogant 16-year-old self told myself. I cursed and swore aloud at what on God's green Earth was I doing driving *toward* a tornado??

I screeched into our driveway at the exact same moment as the brunt of the storm hit. I saw a tree in my front yard bend over and touch its branches to the ground just before everything went under water. The car rocked in place, but didn't tip over when the burst of wind and rain hit the VW like a tidal wave.

"Now what do I do," I thought. Here I was, the last place I'd ever wanted to be—in a car, in a tornado, and I couldn't see anything. It was like I was in a drive-through car wash. I saw a glimmer of light pierce through the wall of water on my windshield, and I knew that my parents had opened the garage door for me to drive in. However, it was the wrong garage door, but it didn't matter because I couldn't see anyway. I decided to make a run for it.

I opened the door and was blasted by wind stronger than anything I'd ever experienced before and I ran the ten feet into the open garage where my relieved parents were standing. I was sopping wet. I looked like someone had just thrown me into a lake and pulled me out again. I was furious.

"WHY THE HECK DID YOU MAKE ME COME HOME?" I yelled. "I was perfectly safe where I was, and you made me drive toward a tornado. Were you trying to get me killed?"

At that moment, the storm blew past and the wind ceased, and they both burst into relieved laughter.

"No, really, are you people insane??" I demanded.

"Well, I guess I just wanted to know you were safe," my mom replied.

"I could have died! And now I'm sopping wet!" I exclaimed in disgust.

"We're sorry," my dad chuckled.

Geez. Parents.

Knowing firsthand the terror that a tornado can deliver, I have absolutely no desire to experience that again. It's my understanding that a tornado is peanuts compared to a hurricane. As I drove along the wasted Florida landscape, it was plain that this was true. Mile after mile of devastation riddled the roadsides as I turned slightly north toward Alabama.

I stopped at the first rest area in Alabama and realized that I had entered the South a ways back. The formal brick structure just screamed southern hospitality. Sure enough, inside the Federalist building there was even an attractive older southern belle volunteer behind the information desk with a drawl as slow and long as molasses. I suspect she remembered Scarlett O'Hara from their cotillion. Considering I had just spent the past few hours pondering the repression and plights of African American rights in the mid-20th century South, I felt somewhat uncomfortable in this plantation-like setting. It felt...wrong. I felt like a Connecticut Yankee at a rebels' Civil War reenactment.

All that being said, the place was very lovely for a rest area, and "Melanie" was very helpful and cheerful. If only they were serving mint juleps on the veranda, I might have stopped a while, but alas, I was merely passing through this time. I wanted to get to Montgomery before dark. For the first time I was in a hurry because I could smell home—not because I had a schedule to keep. It was still two days away, but I was aching to sleep in my own bed once again.

I pulled into the lovely city of Montgomery well before dusk and found a very clean and pleasant motel very quickly. I was anticipating a breezy check-in, and then I was going to grab a quick dinner and hit the hay early so I could get on the road at sunup.

"Ya'll bumerly flemexion, chat?" the desk clerk said.

"I beg your pardon?" I asked.

"Ya'll bumerly flemxion, chat?" she replied.

I had no idea what she was saying to me. However, I did know that she was speaking English, and that the inability to communicate fell squarely upon my ears. She had the thickest Southern drawl I'd ever heard in my entire life.

To this day, I can't figure out what she said, but I vividly remember how incredibly stupid I felt. I suspect she was just asking something like, "King bed or double?" but my pea-sized brain just couldn't process very quickly. I'd never come in contact with a dialect that was so strong that I couldn't follow along—well, except years ago when I was in Liverpool, England, and I was speaking with a Scotsman. That man stood in front of me and insulted me in English to my face and I didn't know it. Everyone around me understood him and was laughing their butts off, but to this day I don't know what he was saying. This was the same situation, except I was in America this time, and it was completely unexpected. Other than North Dakota, this was the only place I heard a very distinct regional dialect. Maybe Steinbeck was right? Maybe dialects are disappearing after all.

After I had the poor clerk repeat her comment as slowly as if she was speaking to a French student with only one semester of English under his belt, I finally caught on and she managed to check me in. Once I found myself tucked into my nice, quiet, warm bed, I cuddled with Judy and started to think about what was going to happen after the trip. It was hard to remember my routine life of waking up to the alarm, going to work, sitting at my desk all day, going home and maybe doing some laundry or reading a book before turning in early to get up in the morning and do it all over again. I did enjoy my work, and I really liked the people I worked with, but that all seemed so long ago. I was a different person then. Back then, I hadn't seen the Can Pile, or the Space Needle, or the French Quarter. Now I had. It felt strange to think of going back. Unable to resolve my confused emotions, I eventually dropped off.

Montgomery, Alabama, to Wytheville, Virginia
Monday, October 18, 2004

I woke up, loaded the van, took Judy for a saunter around the parking lot, and got on the road early. Even though I was eager to get home, I decided to take a small detour off the main artery and touch my feet into a couple of states I'd never been to. I still stuck to main highways, but since I had never been in any states south of Pennsylvania and east of Ohio, I now had the chance to knock most of the remaining states in the lower 48 off my lifetime list. If I picked up Georgia, South Carolina, Tennessee, North Carolina, Virginia, and Maryland, I could proudly state that I had been in 47 of the lower 48 states, with Kentucky being the lone holdout. (I finally knocked off Kentucky in January 2008, when I was returning home from my grandmother's funeral, and my flight transferred at the Cincinnati airport—which, oddly enough, is technically located in Kentucky.)

This day was memorable only in its banality. I wanted to be home, home, home. Judy was lethargic and didn't seem well, and I wanted to get her to her vet. I drove as quickly as I could, and therefore, sadly took in very little of my surroundings. It was raining all day and I stopped as briefly as possible. I even thought maybe I could just soldier straight through until I got home, but by late evening, I was exhausted. By the time I stopped for the night, I had traveled through six states. It had been weeks since I was in states that small. It was just another reminder that I was almost home.

I finally ended the uneventful day in Wytheville, Virginia. The rain had cast a gloom over the pretty area, and I suspect I would have been much more excited to explore the vicinity if it was (a) sunny; (b) a month earlier; and (c) I was just starting out on my journey. I found a clean little motel on the main road, and approached the attractive young man who was smiling from behind the counter in the office. His name badge said, "Travis."

"Do you take pets?" I asked.

"Yes, we do! However, what would you like us to do with them?" he cheekily replied.

Oh ho! Silly motel clerk humor! I was instantly smitten.

Travis cheerily set me up in a fine room by the pool and I slopped through the rain back to the van. I eased Judy out of the passenger seat and she slowly took a walk around the parking lot.

Judy was sick. That much was obvious. Just what exactly was wrong, I didn't know. Her fur was matted and her eyes were glassy. She was eating and drinking as usual, and she wasn't vomiting or anything, but it was very clear that she wasn't feeling well at all. Maybe she was just road fatigued? After all, I didn't feel all that well, either. I fed Judy dinner, petted her for a while; and then she sighed a heavy sigh, turned around a few times, laid down on the bed, and promptly fell asleep. I, however, couldn't sleep. I tucked myself into bed and tried to wrap my brain around the fact that this was my last night on the road. I felt depressed.

Tomorrow night, the whole trip would be only a memory. How long it had taken to plan this journey, how much money and energy did I spend on it, and how arduous had it been at times...yet it seemed to be too early for it to be over. The idea of returning to my normal routine seemed so foreign. Traveling was my norm now. Could I really go back to work in a week? And what exactly had I learned from this jaunt? Did I really have a story to tell? Is that all there is? The big picture snuck up on me once again, and upon its arrival, it took away whatever wind was left in my sails. Mainly, I was just exhausted and I wanted to sleep for days, but I couldn't turn off my brain. Maybe if I watched a movie, I could get myself out of my head? Holy cow, had it really been almost a month since I'd seen a movie? No wonder I was so depressed.

I flipped on the television to see if there was an old movie on. It didn't matter what it was, and if it was one I'd seen before, even better. I love movies. There's nothing better than settling in for a couple of hours to spend time with old friends like Cary Grant, Humphrey Bogart, and William Powell. As I started thinking about movies that always perk me up, I realized I would be blessed if Steve Martin was able to drop in for a visit—*Roxanne*, *LA Story*, or *Dirty Rotten Scoundrels* would have been a perfect antidote to my rain-sodden depression. Doris Day, Rock Hudson, and Tony Randall would be very pleasant faces to see, as would Peter Sellers, Kevin Costner, Ben Stiller, Hugh Grant, or Audrey Hepburn. Suddenly hopeful, I flipped through channel after channel, but I found nothing that looked promising. All I could find were crime dramas, sci-fi apocalyptic movies, and news broadcasts. It's really no wonder why people are so depressed and angry these days, if this sort of negative viewing is their only entertainment options. Finally, I found myself watching an episode of a show called *Monster House*, which was a reality show, and watched a crew of people also go out on a limb and take a chance to improve their lives by accepting a challenge of remodeling an old jail into a break room for Compton, California, police officers. They accomplished what they set out to do, even though at times it definitely looked like they might not make it. It was surprisingly inspiring, and I fell asleep with the realization that no matter what the future holds, if I give 100% toward my dreams, I know I will ultimately succeed—even if I fall short of my projected goal. The joy and passion in life is in the striving for your dreams, not in accomplishing them. Accomplishing dreams is merely a bonus to the rewards of trying, and what an amazingly reassuring thought that was. I slept soundly.

Last Day
Tuesday, October 19, 2004

The rain had abated, but thick fog lingered over the little motel in Wytheville. Today was the last push towards home. It was a long, 11-hour drive, but I knew I'd make it home in one shot. My dad always said he's able to drive longer when he knows he's going to be home, and he's right. It's hard to stop for the night when you're only two hours from your own bed—no matter how tired you might be. So I was happy I got an early start.

I eagerly popped into the motel office, hoping to perhaps see my good-humored new crush, Travis, but alas, a new clerk was on duty. I quickly paid my last motel bill and pointed Roxie towards home.

The remainder of the day was broken down into three memorable events. The first was early in the day, when through the fog, I suddenly spotted a horse-drawn carriage slowly traversing across a bridge crossing the highway about three quarters of a mile ahead. I did a double take and slapped myself to be sure I wasn't dreaming, and I wasn't. At first, I thought I had been reading too much Sherlock Holmes and that road delirium had officially set in, but then I realized that this was Amish country. It was so hauntingly beautiful—a black horse and carriage silently materializing out of the mists—that I was dumbstruck at the sight. The horse's head slowly bobbed up and down as it effortlessly and tirelessly walked on its appointed path. The covered carriage hid its occupants from the wandering eye of local travelers, and it shimmied as it hit tiny bumps in the road. The whole production was so surreal in its surroundings of high-speed motorists and multi-lane highways that it looked like a scene straight out of a Hollywood major motion picture. I found my eyes searching for Harrison Ford.

The second memorable event was a convoy of trucks that I stumbled upon in central Virginia. There was a line of several trucks carrying—I don't know what. After over three weeks on the road, I'd seen all sort of cargo—manufactured homes, logs, horses, pigs, cattle, army jeeps, and the standard enclosed food and consumable goods semis, but I'd never seen any trucks that looked like giant medicine pills. These weren't the traditional "Hazardous Materials" trucks transporting propane, gasoline, or other fluids. These weren't labeled at all. They were just huge white, pill-shaped trailers. One was covered with a sort of tarp. It was very eerie seeing giant Contact capsule cruising down the freeway in the rainy mist.

The third memorable event eclipsed the previous two by leaps and bounds. Around dinnertime, I found myself in Pennsylvania. I exited the freeway in pursuit of a fast-food establishment where I could grab a quick meal.

The rain stopped.

Angels sang.

Rays of light from heaven above burst through the cloud-covered sky.

Hallelujah and praise the Lord! There, at the end of the exit ramp was a Long John Silvers restaurant.

As common as LJS is to a lot of people in this fine country, I haven't eaten at one since I left Nebraska. I was under the impression that they were Midwestern restaurants, much like Taco Johns or Runzas, and to see one so far east was mind blowing. I have since found more of them even closer to home, but on this particular day, it was a tremendous shock and delight! I scurried into the restaurant and ordered up a seafood sampler with lots of hush puppies. Suddenly I was 12 years old again, except this time I ate everything on my plate.

Around about 8:00 p.m., I turned onto my home street. The neighborhood was dark and quiet, and my yard was littered with fallen leaves. All the crowds who were there a month ago to toast my send-off were long gone. I turned off Roxie's motor for the last time, let Judy back into the yard, shuffled up the back steps, and unlocked the door. The house was cold and dark. I flicked a light switch and noticed the dirt on the floor. Of course. I hadn't cleaned before I left. I fed Judy and grabbed a quick snack for myself before unloading the van for the final time. I was so tired. I just dumped everything in the middle of the living room to sort through in the morning. After a quick walk-through of my beloved and missed home, I climbed the stairs, and collapsed exhausted and gratefully into bed.

"And that's how the traveler came home again." ¬John Steinbeck, *Travels with Charley.*

PART THREE

Postscript

A couple of days later, I found myself rested and firmly entrenched in my life again. My house was clean, laundry was washed and put away, and I was getting excited about seeing my work friends once again. Judy had taken a trip to the vet and found out that she had a serious skin infection under one of her legs, but after a few doses of antibiotics, she was on the mend. I had signed up for some film editing classes so I could figure out what to do with the video footage from the trip, and I was re-connecting to friends and family. All in all, my reentry into normal life again was progressing smoothly.

I found myself sitting in my home office wondering why I didn't feel very different than before I left. Why was it so easy to adjust back into my day-to-day world when I know I was vastly changed from the girl who left it a month earlier? After all, I had done something amazing—even by 2004 standards. I was a single woman who traveled around the country and back and I never set foot in a bank. I had strayed so far outside my comfort zone that just a week earlier I was having an emotional meltdown in an Albuquerque motel. Yet here I was grocery shopping and raking the lawn just like I'd never left.

Travels with Charley is anticlimactic in that way as well. Steinbeck left on a search to rediscover America, but the reader ultimately learns more about John Steinbeck. I left to discover history—to search for some tangible connections to Steinbeck's journey—but only returned to myself. Sure, I felt changed in a way. I felt stronger, more secure, and more confident that I could get through anything I needed to get through, but did I feel profoundly altered? No.

And what of this country that somehow managed to elude both John Steinbeck and myself? Is there a unifying thread that connects all its inhabitants to each other? Laws, language, and culture weave us together, but are the people in California the same as the people in North Dakota or the Deep South? I believe they are. But are they alike because of our nationality, or because of our humanity? I believe the latter.

Steinbeck was right when he said that Americans are more alike than different. So what defines an American? Not geography. Our country has practically every type of climate from the Köppen classification. Not religion. We've got them all. Not politics. We're as divided on politics as any country. Not race. We're a melting pot.

I think it's the freedom. Regardless of all the issues that are currently flowing around about restrictive rights regarding sexual orientation, or gender, or race, when you get down to it, we all have the sense of entitlement to freedom. Freedom to think the way we want to. Freedom to speak the way we choose. Freedom to work and love and live on our own terms. In this freedom, however, there is also the desire for fairness. Justice. The worthy live good lives, and the wicked are punished. The guy in the white hat always wins in the end, or at least we really want him to.

That sense of optimism of the possibility of an ideal state is, I think, uniquely American. We may not achieve Utopia, but by golly, we're gonna try. And quite frankly, I think that's pretty swell.

Some things have changed in the years since I finished my trip, and some things have not.

On June 21, 2007, the deconsecrated Lutheran church that housed Holy Smokes BBQ in Hatfield, MA, burned to the ground. There was much mourning from those of us who grew to depend upon their mouth-watering chicken wings and spicy mac-n-cheese.

Brenda Gilchrist is still living in her home on Deer Isle. Life is little changed there even now. I have visited her since my 2004 trip, and we exchange Christmas cards every year. She is one of the dearest people I've ever met, and I'm so thankful this trip introduced me to her.

The Chaffee Café still offers excellent directions in North Dakota. Swing by on your way to The Can Pile.

Mount St. Helens never did re-erupt in any dramatic way. On July 10, 2008, the 2004 eruption was officially declared extinct.

The 2004 election was won by George W. Bush. It was as close as the 2000 election and it took several weeks after election night to determine who had won.

In April 2005, the Wilbur Franz Elementary School was awarded status on the National Register of Historic Places. Months after that, the building was severely damaged when Hurricane Katrina decimated the district. Thanks to Ruby Bridges and other dedicated folks, a new renovation of the building commenced in fall of 2010.

On August 16, 2009, my dearest friend and fluffy travel companion, Judy, gently passed away from kidney failure at the ripe old age of 15. She was such a good girl and she lived a long and happy life. I was so fortunate to be able to share it with her. She was the love of my life.

Looking forward...

In late 2009, a four-year-old red-merle, rescue Aussie who has one blue eye and one blue and brown eye, who goes by the name of Topper, entered my life. He's a little crazy, jumps on people like a battering ram, and spins in a circle when he gets excited, which is often. He likes other dogs, sticks to me like glue, and loves riding in the car.

Judy would have hated him.

Judy
1994 - 2009

ACKNOWLEDGEMENTS

I want to thank James Brown and Kathleen Cain Nastrom for selflessly donating their time and extensive artistic talents, and for helping me retain my sanity through the bulk of the journey. Thank you from the bottom of my heart for your courage, faith, and patience.

For pre-trip preparations and equipment, I want to thank Paul Lawrence, the Yale Digital Media Center for the Arts, and the staff at the Yale University Art Gallery. I want to thank the many people on the journey who opened their homes, resources, and hearts to me: Eastern Long Island Kampgrounds, Brenda Gilchrist, Holy Smokes BBQ and Whole Hog House, Matthew Salewski, Tami Cabrera and Muddy Paws Cheesecake, The Chaffee Café, Ann Roehl, Lisa and Nik Sten, The National Steinbeck Center, Chuck Nastrom, Erin Eisenbarth, Vinh Phan, and Lance Volland. Ohio—thanks for the constant butt kicking.

For post-production work above and beyond the call of friendship, I want to thank Kevin Stramer for his beautiful book design and the fabulous airbrushing he did on my crow's feet, to Lauren Baratz Logsted for her excellent proofreading skills and blurb which will help this book fly off the shelves, and to the Icelandic computer super genius, Pall Thayer, for salvaging the TWJ photos off of a c. 2000 HP computer powered by Windows ME operating system with neither Ethernet port nor writable CD options.

I want to especially thank Treden Wagoner for his unfailing enthusiasm from initial idea through finished project. Your editing skills have saved me from ridicule, your TravelswithJudy.com web page dazzles the world, and your humor is unmatched. By my estimation I now owe you a kidney, should you ever need one.

Thank you Mom and Dad for helping me get on the road, keeping me moving, welcoming me home, and believing in me when I doubted myself.

I want to thank all my family, friends, and supporters throughout this whole harebrained idea. I couldn't have done this without your support and unfailing ear to listen to me whine for literally years. I do owe all of you a drink at least—party date to be determined.

I want to thank Ruby Bridges and Norman Rockwell for inspiring me to bravery.

Oh, and thank you, John Steinbeck. You rock.

Made in the USA
Charleston, SC
23 April 2013